Praise for ~~Coffee~~ ...

"These motivational metaphors flow like the sweet specialty coffee we sip. Barney's words push me as I read, into a calm and steady mindset to take on the day."

*— **Joey Stazzone**, CEO of Café' Kreyol, coffee hunter, humanitarian, founder of Buy a Tree Project.*

"Much like the one she represents, Rita has a way of taking elements and bringing them to life in her storytelling. If you are interested in a read that puts the texture on the walls, this is it. Her creativity shines brightly through these pages. Well done, Rita. Well. Done."

*— **Elijah Tindall**, writer, speaker, comedic storyteller*

"*Unconventional, unique, transparent, authentic,* and *adventurous* are just a few words that come to mind when describing our dear friend Rita! One of our favorite things about Rita is that she is comfortable being the woman God has called her to be. Full of life, energy, and passion, she has pursued and embraced every opportunity and possibility to make a difference in the world around her. She has lived through the joys, the messiness, the ups and downs of life—being true to herself, knowing life is a journey of grace not perfection. Rita is a brilliant writer, and this book is full of wisdom, personal life lessons, and experiences that will challenge you to keep learning and growing in grace as you enjoy the life God has called you to live."

— *Dr. Johnny & Tonya Roby,*
inspirational and motivational speakers
and coaches

Coffee
Talk

Coffee Talk

Food for
the soul

Fuel for
the journey

Rita Barney

MEDIA.COM

Coffee
Talk

Published by
Illumify Media Global
www.IllumifyMedia.com
"We bring your book to life!"

Library of Congress Control Number: 2021911049

Paperback ISBN: 978-1-947360-84-6
eBook ISBN: 978-1-947360-85-3

Typeset by Art Innovations (http://artinnovations.in/)
Cover design by Debbie Lewis

Printed in the United States of America

Acknowledgement

To Poppa Bear, who no doubt has had plenty of practice walking in grace after saying I do at the altar many years ago. For his love, for his patience and encouragement to walk in my moxie, I am forever grateful.

Contents

Preface

Life lived. Stories told. Grace found. We all understand what life is. We've all lived to tell a wild tale or two, but grace? What is grace?

I love the stories my life tells. Somewhere along the way, a dream seed was planted deep inside my soul. I didn't see it at first. I certainly didn't recognize the growth pattern that was taking place. I did not understand for a long time that darkness could be my friend and was no different than deep in the earth where seeds begin to sprout and roots began to form.

I was fascinated with telling stories and on social media, I could tell stories. Never mind if many people read them. I wrote anyway. Some I posted to share. Some I tucked away for safekeeping. I could not explain why. I just did. I wrote. And that seed grew. And it matured and it began to push its way out of the darkness as it found its value. Hence, this book was born.

I am a woman of faith. I believe we all have a purpose, that all things are possible to those who believe, and that we all are in need of grace. Now, I'm not here to push my Christian beliefs nor to throw up a lot of religious bile but to simply remind everyone who dares read my straightforward, down-to-earth mini stories, that they have value and purpose.

I am also here to introduce you to the gift of grace. Grace, it's forgiveness of our mistakes when we don't deserve it. It pulls us out of the murk and the mire whenever we get stuck, and never, ever brings condemnation upon us when we've missed the mark.

Grace, it releases us from the chains of guilt all the while teaching us to forgive.

Heck, I didn't even realize the main topic of this book would be grace until I pulled out the ponderings I had tucked away and saw that grace, like valuable silk thread, had been woven through every page. Grace had shown up, ever so radiantly, surrounding me with the truth that it had something to say. And it had chosen me to say it.

This book is about grace. And how could we find grace without God, the grace giver, because you are loved, just the way you are.

1

The Espresso Factor

Diamonds don't really come from coal as the myth says. I'm not much of a scientist, so I googled and found out that both coal and diamonds are formed from carbon. The difference is, diamonds are formed from a purer carbon than coal, are subjected to extreme pressure and heat, bringing the carbon to crystallization. Thus, giving us a diamond.

I like to think I'm a coffee whiz kid. I'm not, but I like to pretend I am. I do know a little about it, however. Inside Café Paradee, in my little city of Woodward Oklahoma my specialty is espresso drinks. So it stands to reason I would have a fancy, high-powered espresso machine, right?

To make any espresso drink, I fill the puck with ground espresso, tamp it, adjust it into its proper place, tap the brew button, and out comes a dark, rich caffeinated goodness.

One can only achieve the most perfect shot of espresso if and only if the proper technique is used, and if the machine is calibrated correctly. The temperature of the water must be between 196 and 205 degrees Fahrenheit, and the pressure at 8 to 9 atmospheres. The hot water is forced through the ground espresso, extracting the savory nectar from the ground bean. Without the heat and extreme pressure, the finished product would be subpar.

Like the unadulterated carbons that form diamonds or the transparency trade, organic Arabica espresso I serve daily inside the coffee shop, it's not the heat and pressure that makes us dull, weak, and mediocre, it's the lack of it. When the heat comes and the pressure is on, it's what we do with the elements that determines the outcome.

At the end of each short chapter is a section called the Espresso Factor where I ask you questions that hopefully will turn the heat up and put pressure on you to think deeper than you ever have before. I want to be like my espresso machine and provide the right amount of pressure and heat to help you to grow and flourish in your journey. I want above all else for you to prosper and be in good health, even as your soul: your mind, your will, and your emotions prosper.

There's a diamond in you. Your journey is brilliant. You are strong and rich and full of goodness. Sometimes, it just takes a little calibrating, extra heat, and a bit more pressure to bring it to fruition.

Thank you for joining me for *Coffee Talk* and participating in the Espresso Factor.

2

IT'S THERE, CAN YOU SEE IT?

The Espresso Factor

You Were Made
for Such a Time as This

What do you want to be when you grow up?

I believe we all are born knowing our purpose. If we'll just listen to its heartbeat and follow the rhythm, we'll find our path leading us to our destiny.

Take our firstborn daughter TeNeil, for instance. Her life as a tiny dancer began at the age of three. Prancing about in her pink ballet slippers and tutu, she danced her heart out to Chicken Fat and the Hokey Pokey.

At six years old she attended a class in our capital city. That weekend she got a glimpse of her future.

The professor from one of the top dance schools in the nation presided over the class. I had never been exposed to dance schools, or dance lessons for that matter, but I was in awe as I saw how graceful and accomplished the teacher was as she led her class with both freedom and discipline.

I'll never forget it as long as I live; TeNeil coming out of class with excitement in her voice and eyes gleaming.

She said to me, "Mom, when I get big, I'm going to go to this school and Ms. Rowan is going to be my teacher."

Now, I believe you'll agree that most parents would laugh and dismiss this kind of elation, saying, "children that young simply get caught up in the moment of euphoria." Many did not hide well their skepticism when, as TeNeil grew, she continued to talk about how exciting it would be when she was a student at Oklahoma City University.

You must understand that we were full-time farmers/ranchers at the time, on a pretty tight budget, and twenty-five miles from the closest dance studio. However, we believed where there was a will there was a way and that God had a plan.

We did a lot of traveling, even to our capital city, which was two hours away, to give her the best possible chance of fulfilling her aspiration, and we never, ever told her it was impossible. We let her talk and dream and devise. And we told her "all things are possible."

And the day did come. During her senior year of high school the letter of acceptance arrived, along with a promised scholarship. The rest is history. She now owns her own dance company and writes allegories put to music with messages of love and grace, overcoming trials and finding ones purpose. She is choreographer to them all and continues to teach daily, not only the art of dance but also integrity, fortitude, and kindness as she lives out her destiny. She saw her purpose early, and we backed her all the way.

It saddens me as I listen to a plethora of women tell me their life story; how they feel unfulfilled, unworthy, lost without knowing their purpose The number is too high.

There is an over abundance of women peering over the fence at other people's lives, stressing and striving to fit in. They claim someone else's dream as their own, hoping to have purpose, praying someday it will simply show up on their doorstep like an Amazon Prime package that has been delayed.

Oh, my lovelies, you already have the "it" factor. You were born with it. You can't work for it or beg for it. You can't give it away nor can it be stolen from you. Your only responsibility is to use it.

When you grab ahold of the very thing you were put here on earth to accomplish, peace that bypasses all human understanding will be your friend, your guide, your lifeline.

You were made for such a time as this. Now accept it. Embrace it. Enjoy it.

This is your journey.

——— THE ESPRESSO FACTOR ———

Do you have wishes and dreams you've carried around in your soul since childhood? Take a moment right now and write them down. I dare ya.

It doesn't matter how frivolous or impossible the list may look. Throw caution to the wind.

Your journey isn't about how safe you make it, staying inside your box or making sure your safety net is foolproof. It's about getting a dream and running with it.

Without a vision or dream, people wither away, are subject to depression, and miss out on a heck of a lot of fun.

Go ahead and write down your dreams, so you can . . . Run, Baby, Run!

Believe and You Can Walk on Water

*Faith without muscle power
doesn't get you very far.*

That spring when all looked lost, when our nation was in a pandemic lockdown, when fear began to seep into the foundation of everything we knew . . . that 'thing' I had prayed for, contemplated, daydreamed about daily for a very long time began to manifest itself.

I had verbalized it often, but only to my closest people; negativity was not allowed. I refused to let doubt in. It was my responsibility to protect the dream. I believed and I declared those things that hadn't happened yet, as if they already had, until the day came that they actually existed. And I did a lot of homework.

I kept track of the real estate market and which way it was going in Oklahoma City. I watched what was happening in the housing market in the areas in which I was hoping to buy. Were the neighborhoods increasing in quality and value? Did they appear to be safe? Were people moving in or moving out?

For over two years I waited. And the day came, and as that Friday morning began, I knew the day was here. It was time. I knew what I was hearing: "Get out of the boat."

Putting one leg over the side, I called my realtor friend, and she began the search. You see, Poppa Bear and I live and own businesses in Northwest Oklahoma. I wanted a small cottage in the arts district in Oklahoma City. I knew if I didn't lose hope, my desire would become a reality.

And the day we closed on my Plaza District cottage I wept with joy, knowing a true miracle had taken place on this leg of the journey. I'm trying to put into words how things unfolded. How simply divine this part of the journey was.

The words seem forced. They struggle on the page to hold the true value I intend for them. The only words to find right now are those of encouragement. I want to leave hope on this page. I want to leave a forged trail of aspiration, inspiration, and optimism.

THE ESPRESSO FACTOR

And as cheesy as the old cliche may sound, "If you can dream it and believe it, you certainly can achieve it," I have found it works. Every. Single. Time. Don't be so quick to throw in the towel when your ideas and desires don't manifest themselves overnight. It's all about the timing. Walk in faith and trust the timing.

Abraham waited a multitude of years before he became the father of many nations. And yet, he continued to believe. What are you believing for?

Don't get stale and lazy and begin to nap in the boat. Sometimes there's a lot of rowing to be done first.

It's all about the timing. Simply be ready because when things begin to fall into place, they're gonna move fast.

First of all, do you believe? What exactly do you believe?

Do you believe you can or that you can't?

What preparation needs to take place for one of your dreams to begin to manifest itself?

Come on now. Don't be lazy. Don't think you can sit on the couch and eat popcorn and hot tamales waiting for something to happen or simply lollygag about, hoping things fall into place. Get out the oars and prepare. Start rowing. Don't stay in the shallow water. Go out where it's deep. Do a little muscle work. Get sweaty.

If you'll do what you know to do, the rest will fall into place. Trust me. On one of the most unexpected days, Jesus is going to tell you, "It's time; get out of the boat."

What is your why? What is the purpose of your dream? When it manifests itself, what do you plan on doing with it? Do you even know?

Know your why. Know your what. And one unexpected day, your how will show up and be your guide.

3

GRACE
IS
THE
MEANS

The Espresso Factor

She Had Coffee and Donuts

Because grace already knows about the messes.

I have a quirky, keep-you-in-stitches, Chinese Crested Powderpuff fur kid. Her name is Dior. She's black and white with long flowing people hair. I call her my little designer dog. And, yes, she most definitely can be a bossy, female dominant diva. Those of you who have fur babies will understand.

Dior loves food. Actually, she has no sign of a cut off valve when it comes to snacking. She will eat any food: strawberries out of my spinach feta salad, dill pickles from my Friday night burger, quinoa and stir-fry carrots, and Cheetos. She is a huge fan of Cheetos.

Like I said, she'll eat any food, any time, except fried okra. She's not a fan of okra. Personally, I'm not sure what's not to like about this flour battered crispy goodness, but, turning up her nose, it's a "no thank-you" every time it's offered.

I mean really, as soon as she hears a paper rattle...just in case I was opening a box of my favorite shortbreads, a bag of

Boomchick kettle corn, or maybe a bag of those crispy, crunchy, stain your fingers bright orange Cheetos…she comes flying into the kitchen, her long hair flowing, reminding me a little of the '80s Farah Fawcett do, hoping I'll share a nibble or two.

And she's relentless. Tenacity is her middle name when it comes to begging for a morsel from my plate.

Chinese Cresteds are kinda like half dog, half flying squirrel, or maybe they come from Krypton just like Superman. Who really knows? But there is one thing for sure… they can bound with excitement and effortless, endless energy, flying gracefully into the air, covering seven feet at a time.

Dior can glide from floor to the back of the couch, across to the ottoman, darting in zig-zag form, from one side of the living room to the other like a witchy woman on crack.

Some days, she's a churlish little vamp: bossy, in my face, telling me, her human mom, that she needs attention. Other times I find her standing guard, all haughty and prideful over the leftover particles of chewies she has hoarded away, just in case her gentle giant Labrador brother attempts to so much as glance toward the stockpile.

But in his aging canine soul, he extends grace, because he loves her.

Some days she reminds me of me, trying to control my life on my own terms: flailing about like a madwoman attempting to keep all my ducks in a row, hoarding my self-proclaimed prized possessions away just in case there is a shortage, guarding my gifts…those talents and spiritual endowments, my natural abilities, my savvy and skills.

Some of them I have never had to work for. Some were simply gifts; little gold nuggets handed to me from my Creator because I am loved.

In times past I have stood guard like a junkyard watchdog in case a fellow human might play the thief and I would lose the things I was convinced my identity was connected to. But then I found grace . . . because I am loved. And grace covers me when fear shows its ugly head, when the naughtiness seeps from my soul, when I do those things I ought not do because I am human, and humans will act and react and speak when it is best we remain still and silent.

Some time back, we made a road trip to Oklahoma City. If at all possible, when spending the night away from home, we reserve a pet friendly Airbnb so the pups can come along.

Early Saturday morning, we set off for the weekend. The pups were in their reclining positions, Poppa Bear and I had a bag of locally made donuts, and the Yeti was filled with my fresh brewed Haitian coffee.

We nibbled on a couple different flavors of the pastry goodness, then wrapped up the leftover pieces, saving them for a midday snack. I tucked them in a side pocket of the Jeep console, and never thought any more about it.

Later that day, needing to restock a few things for the coffee shop, we made a quick run into Sam's, leaving the pups alone for only a few minutes. The weather was crisp and cool, so the pups were more than comfortable waiting in the Jeep.

When we returned, we found Hooch sleeping, as usual, waiting patiently for our return. Dior, on the other hand, was perched upon the console on guard duty. It was a truly typical scenario. I waved at Dior, she responded with a tail wag and showed her pearly whites in her classic canine smile fashion as if to say, "I'm the innocent one. I didn't do a thing."

I wondered what's up. Upon opening the door, I found what appeared to have been nothing less than a possible visit from a Tasmanian devil. The tissue paper the donuts had been wrapped in was shredded and scattered all over the front bucket seats. The remaining bits of the donuts were obviously never to be found.

My Yeti cup, which still had coffee in it, had been resting in the cup holder was now topsy-turvy inside my favorite vintage leather travel bag that was setting on the passenger side floor. The items inside the bag were now swimming in cold coffee.

Dior stood on the console, yawned nonchalantly, pretending nothing had happened. Her big brother sat silently in the back seat simply watching the fiasco go down. It was obvious he was not getting involved.

The front seat of the Jeep was a mess, but what can I say?

The girl wanted coffee and donuts.

I chuckled to myself, patted her on the head, cleaned up the mess, and found grace . . . because she is loved.

As sure as we live and breathe it is inevitable that messes are going to be made. We're going to leave a paper trail of some kind leading right to the crime scene. It's part of the journey, actually. Sometimes we can't help ourselves. Sometimes we get caught up in the moment; we lose our head, make wrong choices, and our life gets muddled.

Oh heck, it seems as if some of us have spent entire seasons living in muddled conditions. But then there is grace. Like Hooch, God's grace sits watching, knowing the outcome cannot be good, but never tattling or bringing condemnation. He cleans up our messes, pats us on the head, and simply smiles. Because we are loved.

—— THE ESPRESSO FACTOR ——

Grace. It's not a license to continue in our muddled condition, it's forgiveness for the mishaps, poor choices, and messes we've made. Period. Grace covers it all.

Our journey is to be lived out loud not in the shadows of guilt and condemnation.

Are you living in the shadows of your past messes? It's time to face them. Address them by writing them down. Every last thing that haunts you and makes you feel judged and holds your soul captive. What is it you need grace over right now, to bring you out of the darkness so you can be free of your own prison bars?

Now, allow God's grace to hug you, clean up the mess, and unlock those guilt chains. Grace is forgiveness, because you, my dear, are loved.

Grace Is Sufficient for Me

Overcoming the Wonder Woman syndrome.

I positioned myself in the middle of my efficient kitchen to start my daily responsibilities. My list of duties had been previously downloaded in my brain. I went from station to station prepping, cleaning, baking, rearranging. And then I froze.

There was no doubt, I had shut down, resembling an upright corpse, as I reached for the handle of the large refrigerator that stood in front of me. It was like my brain died, and I couldn't think. I became an empty creature struggling to remember what was next on an overpacked agenda. And I got nothing. A big fat zero.

Stress will do that to a person. Shut you down. Render you impotent of your senses. Panic began to rise inside my soul, and I felt alone with my undone tasks.

After what seemed like an eternity, a strong, yet calming, promising voice resounded in my soul admonishing me that grace was all I needed at that time. I breathed in, slowly filling my lungs with invigorating air. My mind was refreshed with an assurance I was not alone.

I was one person. I would do what one person could do and let the rest fall where it may. I would grant God permission to extend His grace, and I would allow His gift to guide my journey and remove the guilt that had begun to grow because I was failing at being "Wonder Woman." My personal super hero tools seemed to be insufficient for the day's tasks. Wasn't I supposed to be the rescuer, the doer, the defender, the guardian? It was because of my stubbornness and my super-hero perspective, that, that day I found I was the one needing to be rescued. I needed to be redeemed from my own perturbation. I was reminded that I am a human. And humans have limits. We were designed to have limits.

I had come to the end of myself, admitting that one person alone was not capable of prepping for three days' worth of entrees, along with the needed desserts, sauces, and extras, for even a small thirty-seat café, especially in twenty-four hours. It was next to impossible, but with grace comes peace and with peace comes a knowing that everything is going to be alright.

And I clung to that same grace, two days later, even as the nurses wheeled Poppa Bear into exploratory surgery at 6:30 a.m. I clung to grace as all motion around me blurred, and the specialists began to prepare for the unexpected, emergency quintuple bypass to repair his heart.

We did not see this one coming. This was one of those startling bumps in the road.

And as I sat waiting on others to orchestrate this process, I began to meditate on the obvious: I could not play Wonder Woman today. In fact, I could not play Wonder Woman tomorrow.

I was in a position that I had to trust others with Poppa Bear's health. After all, they were the experts in their field, just as God's grace is the ultimate expert, knower, comforter, peace giver, way maker . . . my joy. With this acceptance, His grace is sufficient for me.

———— THE ESPRESSO FACTOR ————

I was not designed to play the part of Wonder Woman. You were not created to fight off the albatrosses that come to overwhelm you and plunder your journey.

Wonder Woman is fiction. She is a fantasy found only in comic books. Trying to fill the shoes of a fictional character keeps us from living our best life. And it puts us in chains.

How many times in your daily life do you try to play the part of Wonder Woman?

How many times a day do you feel overwhelmed by your tasks and guilt-ridden because you can't fill her shoes. It's time you allow yourself freedom from the Wonder Woman syndrome.

Put a name to the chains that keep you in bondage to this fantasy.

In what ways do you feel responsible and pressured into playing the part of a superhero?

Write down a couple of ways you can tweak your life toward more peace. Maybe you've already pared down your schedule as much as possible yet the guilt of not doing enough is still there. Where is this guilt coming from?

Is the source another human or from yourself? The Giver of grace wants you to be free.

Now write a few sentences addressed to the gift of grace asking for help with the things you cannot handle on your own. Forgive yourself for not being able to handle it all. Now, give thanks for your freedom.

Did Someone Say Cat?

*Through the prickly sage brush and clawing
sandburs we will find grace.*

I woke as the early summer sun began to peer through our bedroom window. I stretched out into a long yoga stretch, then rose, my eyes still heavy with sleep. Fumbling about, I searched for my flip-flops and glasses.

The dogs of course, were leaping and yipping and doing the dog kinda gymnastics they do every morning when it's time to venture outside for their business.

I had intended on waking early. Time was ticking. The moonflower was calling my name. It is a night bloomer that puts on its best show when the moon shines its brightest, but as soon as the sun hits its large, coarse, primitive leaves and fragile, white lily-shaped blooms it closes up tight and snoozes during the heat of the day.

I had checked on it at 11:00 the previous night, but it only showed signs of stirring. I left it dozing but was determined to see it early the next morning as the sun peered over the horizon. I wasn't sure I had ever seen a moonflower before. Poppa Bear had talked about them growing here and there around the farm in his younger years but so much time had passed neither of us had given it much thought, until the day last summer when he was out on his ventures and ran across a lonely plant sleeping among sage brush.

Excited about his find, he collected some of the seeds as a surprise for me. Without me knowing, he carefully planted the seedlings in a select spot and nurtured them for several weeks, waiting for its tiny green sprouts to pop through the soil, mature, and bloom.

This was the morning we had been waiting for, and no, it did not disappoint. I witnessed approximately twenty opened blooms while at least a dozen more remained in their cocoon, abiding for another day.

The atmosphere was surreal. Mr. Bob White and family chatted amongst themselves somewhere in the nearest brush. The Barn Swallows enjoyed their morning breakfast as they swooped through the air snatching up unassuming insects. Crickets tuned up their notorious violins while the dogs sat in the side yard sniffing the fresh morning air. I slumped in my favorite vintage lawn chair, on the wraparound porch, daydreaming and soaking up the perfection of the morning.

Unexpectedly, without any warning, the atmosphere became electric with a screeching bark. I jolted back to reality as I saw our old guy Hooch bolt toward the draw just south of the cabin, followed by the agile Crested, leaping over and through the rough terrain. Now, Hooch has never cared much for discipline when it came to exercising manners around cats and thus taught the youngest member of the family to be just as rude to the fuzzy feline kind. This morning was no different, except that the cat was no ordinary feral. It was a bobcat every bit as big as the old lab that chased him.

It would probably be a safe bet to say the cat was in its prime and could have whipped the old guy and had Dior for a fast food breakfast.

What was I doing while the chase was on? I most definitely was right smack dab in the thick of it. I had quite the disadvantage from the other three however, for my feet were shod only with my thin, light weight flip-flops. But I crashed through the ugly, clawing sandburs and scratchy wild sagebrush none the less, with only one vision in mind . . . save the pups!

"Hooch! Stop! No! Dior! Stop it now! Bad Dog Stay," I shrieked.

In all the upheaval, I suppose Dior remembered she had never taken the time too pee pee and deciding amidst all the commotion, now was the time, did her thing, which allowed me the ability to catch up with her. All the while, I continued to scold frantically.

As I shooed her back toward the house, she pouted at being made to walk back through the prickly brush. Hooch chased the oversized cat for a few more moments before giving up, deciding the cat was geared to higher speeds.

Dior froze as a sandbur became lodged in her tender paw. Feeling sorry for her, I carried her the rest of the way back to the porch as Hooch limped in beside me after pulling a hamstring. The excitement was over, leaving me with two wounded, long faced, worn out pups on my hands, both needing petted and consoled as we headed towards the porch.

Isn't this exactly like life though? Sometimes we're just minding our own business, enjoying our surroundings—our job, our family, friends, our daily routine—and someone says cat, and all heck breaks loose. We lose our wits, our peace, and sometimes our ability to hear. We begin to chase after an intriguing shiny object to find out later it was only fool's gold.

When the chase is over, we face defeat, we limp back to the comfortable safe zone, licking our wounds, all the while disappointed the chase was a failure and feeling a bit embarrassed because it was.

When the fur kids and I reached the front of the porch, I gave them pets and hugs and fresh water to ease their pain. I could do nothing but love on them and laugh with amusement at their curiosity-driven caper. And I am reminded of grace.

Grace consistently waits for us with open arms, with affection, with understanding when we have been disobedient; charging off into the wilderness to do our own thing. When we've lost our head and made poor choices, when we've gone on wild goose chases, God still loves us. When we've ignored His voice of warning, He is still there with grace. After we've come to our senses and begin licking our wounds, His grace is there. He is loving us, petting us, assuring us all is well again.

It is our Creator's promise: "My Grace is always enough for you, and in your weakness I am able to show you my strength."

Because of grace, there is no need for condemnation, only reassurance we are loved.

——— THE ESPRESSO FACTOR ———

We must surrender to the fact that we're not always going to make good choices.

Case in point, Peter, a hard-working businessman, honest but brash, passionate yet hotheaded, a disciple of Christ. Jesus trusted him. In fact, he was in Jesus's inner circle.

Still, he lost his head when the soldiers came to take Jesus into custody. Jesus told him to stay put, but he overreacted, drawing his sword and cutting off the soldier's ear. Jesus scolded him and healed the soldiers ear. Later on, Peter denied even knowing Jesus.

Jesus called him the rock, even though he continually lost his head.

Has there ever been a time you have lost your head darting off in a direction you knew you shouldn't go, and when you gained your wits, you were embarrassed? Bewildered at your actions?

Write the details of what triggered the rash decision. What kind of mess did you find yourself in? How did you fix it or does it continue to weigh heavily on your heart?

Admit it if you acted irrationally. Ask forgiveness if you wronged anyone. It will set you free.

Have you ever made a mistake that you think might be bigger than God's grace? Did you ever allow yourself to accept God's grace, or are you still carrying condemnation around with you?

Write in your notes: I forgive myself.

If you have walked away free, what was the turning point? And just like I did with my pups, grace will meet you where you are, remove the prickly burs, and nurse your soul back to health.

4

PERCEPTION IS EVERYTHING

The Espresso Factor

Check Your Lens

Don't be a Maxine.

I admit it. There are those times my middle name could be Crotchety; you might even call me a curmudgeonette. Yep, every now and then it appears that Maxine from the comic strips might have been my mentor.

I'm not a fan of the Debbie Downer Club. I like to believe I practice what I preach and that I am a testament to my own philosophy for life: Be the light.

In reality, I invariably miss the mark. Sometimes I find myself desperately wanting the sun to shine, but inside my private little world, the forecast is cold and drab and cloudy. Some days my soul wants to bury itself deep under the covers, looking for the same comfort I felt as a child when I was most certain a monster was lurking somewhere in the corner of my room. Other days the laughter refuses to come without a struggle, and my soul strums a melancholy blues tune as if it were debuting on a well-worn stage in a nostalgic, dimly lit, smoke-filled club deep in the South.

Don't get me wrong. I adore jazz. There's something so raw and real and honest about it. But seriously, singin' the blues shouldn't become a lifestyle.

One lazy Saturday while rummaging through a quaint little vintage shop, I found these magnificent turquoise Lucite glasses. It was love at first sight.

The lenses were badly scratched and it was evident someone had definitely gotten a lot of use out of them. My plan was to take them to my local optometrist to have the lenses replaced with my own prescription, so I gladly paid the asking price. Needless to say I was greatly disappointed when the doctor told me the frame had aged poorly and was not strong enough to withstand the heat and pressure it would take to change out the lens. These gems had played their part well, but now they would become a conversation piece resting alongside the many vintage hats lining my bedroom bureau.

As I placed the cat-eye glasses on my dresser, I thought about the previous owner and how she must have thought it was time for a change . . . time to retire the old and purchase a new set of looking glasses.

Maybe it's the same with life: our old view gets scratched and askew, leaving us a bit disgruntled. Maybe when we begin to sing the blues, all we need is a fresh view. Maybe all we need is to change the lens we are looking through.

─────── **THE ESPRESSO FACTOR** ───────

You may laugh when you read Maxine cartoons but viewing your life negatively day after day makes for a sad, lonely, defeated journey. Being positive, finding the nuggets of goodness (even on the worst of days) is like striking a match in the darkness. The more matches we strike, the brighter our world.

Make a list of ten positive things happening in your life today. Yes, I really did say ten. You may be feeling broke, busted, and disgusted, but make a point to look for the good.

Examples could be that you woke up today. The sky is blue today. You have electricity. It's raining and watering the earth. You heard the birds sing. You are loved. Because, you really are loved . . . by me. I can promise you that. That's why I wrote this book. Now, read your list of positive things out loud to yourself every day.

Get a visual as you verbalize the positive. Why? Because verbalizing the positive changes things. Our words have the power to create life or death. The direction you go is up to you.

Like many of you, I've hit some pretty rough spots along the way. I've had close calls with bankruptcy, experienced the death of a granddaughter, faced false accusations, and suffered bouts of anxiety. In order to survive, I've had to learn to allow hope to germinate.

Positivity is the fertilizer that makes hope grow. Believe for the best; focus on the fact that anything is possible if we stay positive and believe.

If your world looks dark, dingy, and gray, check your view. You just might need to change your lens.

Pow* Slam* Whack* Bang* Boom* Bash*

Real life is more like an episode of Gotham
than Leave It to Beaver.

---

*B*am! *Krunch! Zonk! Klonk! Kapow! Whamm! Crash! Ooof!*
Splaat! I remember these words flashing across the TV
screen as Batman and Robin duked it out with the villains of
Gotham City. The mighty superheroes always won. Every episode was predictable, but I invariably felt apprehension each
week, wondering *"What if somehow the duo would fail and Go-*
tham would fall under great siege."

Of course that never happened but the thought was nerve-
racking. After the barrage of blows, with nary a scratch, Batman
and sidekick Robin would speed off toward the Bat Cave,
chuckling with victory, knowing their fair city would sleep
soundly yet another night.

These days, Poppa Bear and I love to watch *Gotham*, a
prequel to the Batman series. I find myself just as intrigued,

still unnerved as in time's past, as I watch these supervillains spread mayhem and evil across the city. So far the police force is winning, but with each new season, I wonder how many more wins are left before the hero, Master Wayne, goes to the Bat Cave, slips into his tights and cape, and speeds off to save the metropolis.

Poppa Bear and I were born and raised in the same rural Oklahoma county. We then raised our kids on the family ranch where he had grown up. After our youngest graduated from high school, to our surprise, the urge to explore a different world began to tug at our souls.

A business opportunity had been presented to us. In fact, two opportunities arose, and we were giddy with confidence that our time to be leaders on an entirely new level and to prosper in ways we had never experienced had come. We sold our business and headed south. We left our home, our family and all we had ever known to expand in a unknown territory.

We set out for adventure.

Now, you must understand, I am married to a rock solid, cowboy; a farmer-rancher-numbers guy whose roots in rural America grow deep. He has never been the "fly by the seat of your pants and let's see what will happen" kind of guy. So when we invested some pretty big bucks in a new company, packed up our favorite things, and moved to a metroplex, it was a miracle. We were transplanted and we wasted no time settling in, working hard both physically and emotionally to allow our roots to deepen. We were determined to bloom where we were now planted. There was no doubt in our minds that this was part of our destiny, and we embraced this unfamiliar leg of the journey.

We had found the perfect historical house to restore and Poppa Bear acquired a great office representing the new company in which he was now part owner. To take care of the latest expenses in our new city, we opened a bank account and began writing checks from the new account. And bloom we did for about six weeks.

Without getting into all the deep, dark, messy poo that we began to step in, I will just say we were left high and dry, accumulating debt caused by others. We had been abandoned by those who we trusted implicitly, and we found ourselves alone in a city we knew very little about. As we looked around us, all we could see was loss. We were broke, busted. and disgusted. And I cried.

BAM!, SLAM,! WHACK,! BANG,! BOOM,! BASH! Where was our Batman, and our Robin?

Wouldn't it be sensational if our lives were like the superhero shows? We face insurmountable obstacles. We fight crime and injustice. We never have to protect our hearts from disappointments because we always win in the end.

Wouldn't it be grand if we lived in a world where rejection and sadness and difficulty were always intercepted before the pain could come?

Wouldn't it be spectacular if our victories were promised and were a sure fire thing, if we never had to deal with the harsh blows of reality, if we were never blindsided by deception and chicanery that leave us retching with emotional anguish, fear, and disappointments? Alas, only in the movies.

In real life, there will be times we are bruised and bloodied by the venomous human tongue. Times we may have been lied to. Times we run smack dab into harsh concrete walls of someone else's devious schemes, when honesty and integrity is our main virtue.

The truth is, if we expose ourselves to love, if we open ourselves up to caring, if we dare to lead and share and be transparent, if we dare take a chance at life at all, there will be days we take unbearable hits, and our world looks as if it has been shattered.

The truth is, we are not superheroes. Batman and Robin do not exist in real life. We do not wrestle with the Joker, Penguin, or Riddler.

What we do grapple with are brutes like brokenness, depression, anxiety, rejection, abandonment, fear, loneliness, and addictions. The solid truth is, hurting people do hurtful things and desperate people take desperate measures.

When we lost nearly everything and were abandoned in a strange city, were we heart broken? Did we face fear each and every morning? Were we angry? The answer is yes, yes, and yes to them all.

However, we knew that if we did not allow ourselves to dwell on all the hits we had taken; —the extra debt, the rejection, even the embarrassment, —we would be okay.

We rallied and went in another direction. Was it easy? Heck no. But the exciting news is, we eventually won.

Because we didn't wait for Batman to show up but made love, grace, and forgiveness our superpowers, healing began to show up in the most unusual ways. In our brokenness, our soul began to thrive. Where there was sorrow, we found joy, and confidence replaced our fear.

It didn't happen overnight, but just like Batman and Robin, Poppa Bear and I began to laugh again because we knew all was well in our fair city . . . and in our soul.

——— THE ESPRESSO FACTOR ———

Nobody ever promised the journey would be a bed of sweet smelling roses. About the time I began to believe it just might be, I discovered with the bed of roses comes thorns. We had been misled, sold a bill of goods.

We think our lives should look like Leave It to Beaver, where there's a white picket fence, where mom cleans house in a well-pressed, cheeky dress, where dinner is always served on time, where mom and dad never have a tiff, and where the Beav and Wally never, ever have a rebellious teenage moment.

But life is not about the picket fence and does not come wrapped up with a tidy bow. It's about the journey as a whole. It's about expecting the best, dealing with the inferior bits, and learning to live with both.

Life is the journey. How you live it is up to you. If you want to live it in a small cardboard box lined with fear, unforgiveness, and offense, it's your choice. However, living inside the box doesn't invalidate the journey. It simply means you live in self-made shackles that keep you from the many adventures along the way.

Were the five years we spent in Texas a cakewalk? Heck no! Did we learn a lot while we were there? You bet we did.

It is simply part of our story. And as I look back, I can say I am grateful for all of it. It means we took a chance. We not only survived, but because we choose to forgive and extend grace to those who had cheated us; because we choose to trust God's word that promises us that all things are possible if only we believe. In so many ways we flourished.

We've all had those times we felt we might not survive. What was your Gotham City moment? What was that thing you have felt betrayed by? Rejected from? Maybe there was a time you felt the floor of your world was dropping out from underneath you. Maybe there was a time hope was slipping away.

Write down what almost killed your soul.

How did you handle that situation? Don't just think about it. Write it down. Be blunt and real with yourself. Did you hold onto unforgiveness, or did you allow God to pull your worn-out, broken-down soul from the battlefield so you could begin to heal?

Did you retreat and hide inside the safe zone, or did your determination and tenacity allow your hope to be restored?

What suggestions do you have for others fighting their own battle?

Learn to fight the good fight of faith because most days our lives are more like Master Wayne's than the Beav's.

Don't Forget to Use the Beeswax

---

*The outside was dry and splintery,
the inside rusty, but sometimes it's our mind
that needs a makeover.*

One of the most recent DIY projects Poppa Bear and I worked on was a late 1800s chest-style icebox. It had been his grandmother's and had been in our barn for years. When we moved from the farmhouse, we took it with us. When we moved again, it found its way in the moving van. And again, for the third time, it was housed in yet another storage facility.

After storing it for forty years, it was time to bring it back to life. The wood was dry and splintered, the inside rusted, and somewhere along its journey someone for some odd reason sawed two inches off the legs on one end, leaving the legs on the other the original height. But we had a vision for this magnificent piece of history. It had spent enough time in the shadows. It was time for it to shine and have a new purpose.

I spent the Memorial Day weekend scrubbing, sanding, oiling, and polishing this old piece of nostalgia with lots of beeswax. Life had taken its toll. It was my job to resuscitate it.

As I worked, I pondered how our minds often run parallel to this old relic. Throughout our own journey, we can find ourselves in a dark place and we experience hard times. We feel forgotten or misused, a bit rusty, and worn out.

Our mind is quick to remind us of the, woulda, coulda, shoulda moments. And then the race is on. Worry shows up ready to entertain. It can be quite the successful hostess and loves to send out invitations to its entire pessimistic tribe, including anxiety and depression. It will continue to do so as long as we allow it to address the invitations. We give our final approval when we lick the stamps.

I faced a challenge recently and had to fight my way back to a healthy, positive mindset. In actuality, the sequence of events was no big deal—until I began to overthink it, which lead to lost sleep, causing me to stress out more, and the cycle had begun.

To stop worry in its tracks and prevent the party from happening, I knew I had to nourish my mind, my will, and my emotions with good stuff. I had to reach for the true Word. I had to spend some time executing TLC to my emotions. To be emotionally healthy I had to kick the negative thoughts to the curb.

And as I pondered this, I discovered a rusty, misused spot hidden deep inside my soul. I could not, I would not ignore the fact that there was still some renewing, some restoring, some polishing that needed to be done.

I had to draw a line in the sand. I would not allow the bumps and bruises from the past dictate my future. It was time to do a little extra sanding and a little more polishing; a bit more reconditioning of my mind was needed.

We all need renewing from time to time. There is nothing weak about refurbishing our perspective. And as we grow as women, we will find in ourselves the strength, the courage, and the tenacity. We must not hide away when we discover poo has shown up, but look underneath the grime for what it really is: life.

Yes, some messes take a little more scrubbing, polishing, and tending to than others, but when the work is done, we'll shine.

The antique ice box was on its way to being completed. To make it functional again, Poppa Bear sawed off the longer legs to match the shorter ones.

I spent hours applying tung oil, polishing, applying beeswax, and buffing then I repeated . . . until I thought my arms were going to fall off. All that was left was a couple of coats of salmon-pink chalk paint to the lid to add a pop of color. Voila! It looked incredible.

As for me personally, I'm working on myself. When the rough spots appear, I refuse to help address the invitations to a party that will only overthrow my destiny. I refuse to lick the stamps for the invitations to be mailed. I choose to be restored and made functional by the renewing of my mind, and that is the beeswax to my soul.

——— THE ESPRESSO FACTOR ———

Rough spots left behind by hurt feelings, rejection, and disappointments are inevitable. We all need a restoration job every once in a while. Without a bit of reconditioning and polish, we become rusty with splinters, not unlike our antique icebox, and our countenance becomes prickly and rough, ugly and worn.

When was the last time you overhauled your soul?

Do you have rough spots that need tending to? Are some spots exceptionally sensitive and painful?

What part of your soul; maybe your mind, or will or emotions need to be overhauled in order for it to be functional again?

Allow your mind to be restored by the washing and sanding and polishing with the truth of grace. Because it is that truth, when you allow it, that really does set you free.

And don't forget the beeswax. It does wonders too.

5

TEND TO YOUR GARDEN

The Espresso Factor

Timing Is Everything

Take care of your roots.

I've been an Oklahoman for all but five of my sixty plus years. I suspect it to be true, that we, here in our Sooner state have some of the most capricious weather anyone has ever seen.

It's never a surprise to me when spring begins to show her sunny disposition, I find not twenty-four hours later she has thrown us into a tailspin with anything from wildfires to cold icy wind and snow.

She can be happy, friendly, and calm one moment, and the next thing you know, she's throwing a temper tantrum like an unpredictable two-year-old testing his momma, trying to find exactly where his boundaries lie.

My friend Gloria has a family owned nursery. I love going into her greenhouses and breathing in the damp soil, the CO_2, and the sweetness of the half-opened blooms. It takes me back to my childhood when helping my dad prepare the soil for his spring planting. It reminds me of his tomato plants, bell pepper seedlings, and the onion bulbs, sitting in one of my mom's kitchen windows, all waiting anxiously to have their roots tenderly placed into the ground, to do what they do best—take root, bloom and produce fruit.

Early every spring I ask Gloria what new annuals she has for sale. Every year she tells me the same thing she has told me for the last umpteen springs. "Rita," she says, "don't buy before the first of April, preferably not before Easter. Those little things will take a hard hit when the temperature drops, and if they survive, their growth will be stunted."

For everything there is a season, not only for my dad's vegetables to be planted, or for me to fill the large, empty clay pots that sit lonely and bare outside my café door, but for us too.

There really is a time for us to be planted. There is an allotted time for us to grow a root system and a time to bloom. There is even a time for us to produce healthy, vital seeds for the next season.

I'm a visionary. I dream big and often, which is a fantastic thing, except for the fact I have a tendency to run right smack dab into my plan, forgetting there is also a season for dreams to come to fruition. Like planting my seasonal annuals before the soil is warm enough, when I rush into a plan, I put my entire design and purpose at risk. Patience is vital.

God's timing is everything. Jumping ahead can be dangerous but procrastination does us no good either. Have you ever been to one of those nursery chains mid-summer when those poor little plants are beginning to shrivel and turn brown? Ugh, it always hurts my heart a little knowing no one cared enough to take them home and tend to their needs.

It doesn't surprise me that my destiny would be revealed slowly, one day at a time, on a need to know basis. I suspect if I knew too much, I would consistently be jumping ahead, stunting my root system, slowing down the bloom production, maybe even preventing seed from being produced for the following season.

For everything, there is a season—to be planted, to develop a sturdy root system, to bloom, and finally, to produce seed.

Be patient.

Your season is coming.

——— THE ESPRESSO FACTOR ———

I have irises and daylilies in my cottage garden, along with a knock out rose bush, lantana, and sunflowers. I have known for a long time, that irises and daylilies are the first to welcome in spring. But the year after we planted the lantana plants, I was convinced they hadn't made it through the tough Oklahoma winter.

By mid spring I was about to head to the local nursery to start the process over when I noticed the little green leafy heads beginning to pop through the soil. The days were consistently warm, and the overhead sun had warmed the soil considerably. My sunflowers woke up a few weeks later.

Each species of flower has its own time to bloom. When I realized this, I could be confident my garden would flourish in due season, and I could stop my fretting about it not producing on time.

For everything there is a time and season. What season are you in?

The toiling season? You can't put good seed into lumpy, unprepared soil and expect it to flourish. Prepare your soil before you plant. Have you done that?

The planting season? Is your seed effective? Have you been generous with your seed, or are you sowing sparingly?

Be aware that we reap what we sow.

Maybe you're in the watering season? The watering season is the season for nurturing. Are you watching over your seed?

Tend to your garden. Tend to your dream. Keep the trash out, deposit fertilizer to your soul, and don't forget to water.

Stop your fretting. Stay diligent and don't fret the process. Your season's coming.

You're about to bloom.

Check Your Soil

Mary Mary quite contrary,
how does your garden grow?

Our little cottage in Oklahoma City has a roomy backyard. A massive, aged pecan tree sits on the west corner
with its well-established branches extending across a big part of
the south end. Various, overgrown bushes line the east fence.
Shade is prevalent and rules what is allowed to grow in this section of the yard.

During a routine inspection to the property before closing,
a leaky sewer pipe was discovered. This find allowed for a new
line to be laid, at the seller's expense, which was a real asset for
us, indeed. But there was a downside.

I stood by while a monstrous backhoe was unloaded. Its
huge tires dug deep into the grassy earth while buckets of soil
were scooped up by an angry metal bucket, baring its teeth,
destroying the vegetation on the entire east side of the yard.
When the job was complete, we were left with piles of dirt,
unfilled crevices, and a disheveled mess.

What we discovered while we labored to fix the unsightly mess was that we could not solely blame the sparseness of the grass on the shade but part of the problem was that the soil was clay: pure black, sticky, clumpy clay.

When it was dry, it was solid as a rock. After an inch of rain, the clay became as slippery as a roller skating rink, and it clung to my galoshes as if Gorilla Glue were part of its DNA.

Now, Poppa Bear is an agronomist, so he understood the problem. Me? Well, I googled to find a solution. It did not work for me when I bought bags of grass seed to be sprinkled lavishly across this wasteland. But alas, my agriculture-minded husband had already told me I would find this to be unproductive.

At first the grass seed baked in the sun then took a river ride into the ditch as a midnight rain broke free from the dark clouds that housed it.

If we wanted a green, lavish yard we must first break up the molecules of soil with our tiller, then add loam, which would make the soil more pliable, disperse the nutrients easier, and help with drainage. And for every thing there is a season. Experts say that the autumn season is the best time for this backyard project to be executed.

I perceive life through a series of allegories so of course, without volition, I naturally correlate gardening with our lives. I had to pause and take note of my own personal soil. Have I been adding the proper nutrients it needs to function at full capacity, adding enough emotional loam to help my soul flourish?

We can hardly pick up a magazine these days without seeing articles written by so-called 'experts' telling us how to improve our physical body. Fitness gurus preach to us on what to eat and what not to eat; instructing us on how to become vegetarians or vegans, how to follow a keto or whole30's diet, even why we should live a gluten or dairy free life. I could go on, but my concern is not so much about the shape of our physical bodies but that many of us are neglecting our soul.

We can't give what we do not have. If our soul is depleted of emotional nutrients, we fail to produce. If we allow our hearts, minds, and emotions to become like clay, even the healthy seeds can't grow. We must tweak our soil with loam: love, positive words, kindness, adventure, and faith.

Poppa Bear and I are gonna feed our backyard clay like soil the compost it needs because we want our yard to produce lush green grass. We want to be able to grow plants favorable even to shade.

We want our yard to be a paradise for those who are in need of a reprieve from their daily routines, just as I envision my life to be an example of peace, encouragement, love, and mercy.

But first, I must check my own soil to see if it is conducive to producing the beatitudes I hunger for.

Check your soil, be mindful of your season, and if need be, add some loam.

THE ESPRESSO FACTOR

Most of us have some form of backyard, a place where we have green grass and plant annuals or perennials. Maybe there's even a vegetable garden or a pecan tree. Some of us may have a concrete balcony with big terracotta pots in which to grow our summer ferns.

No matter the type or way we garden, if we want to enhance our space with living plants, it is our obligation to take care of the soil. Now, I understand that a few of you might hire someone to do your gardening, but the soil still needs tender care.

The point is, we must make our soil our responsibility. What we grow and produce is up to us. We can't blame others if the plants wilt from dehydration. We can't point the finger at the neighbor because their garden is more lush than ours. We can't get mad because there are sandburs growing instead of roses.

Our garden is ours to tend. It's no different with our soul. What we feed it is our decision. We have to be accountable to fertilize and add the nutrients. If we want our soul to be lush and healthy, we have to spend time nurturing it. The choice is up to us.

Is your soul conducive to producing the fruit you'd like others to see?

Scary as it might be, take a hard look and write down what weeds need to be pulled. Make a decision to enhance your soil.

Mary Mary quite contrary, what does your garden grow?

Don't Fear the Darkness

I ain't afraid of no ghost.

I grew up gardening. My dad was more than a hobbyist; he was a pro. We lived on a ten-acre plot, the last house in city limits. Approximately six of the ten acres were set aside for growing vegetables and berries of all kinds and varieties. If it could be grown in the northwest Oklahoma winds and sweltering heat, it was in our garden.

We began the end of February and never stopped until the first autumn frost. It started with buying the seed potatoes, cutting them to have at least one eye to a cube. Then came the root vegetables, such as onions and radishes, and with each new week thereafter came warmer weather and something new to plant. Of course, the asparagus was usually the first of April, and then by May, the race was on to plant, pick, and weed the entire acreage.

I hated gardening. Every single thing about it. Well, except the fresh okra that became copious the latter part of June when the days were long, and the sun brought extravagant heat. It was my job to do the picking.

If you're not from the South, you may not know about okra. It's one of the yummiest vegetables ever to be grown. However, when picking it and nurturing it, one must wear what I will call "a suit of armor." Okra plants, including their leaves, are prickly and with only one touch, will make your skin itch as if it were on fire. On the days I was to do the picking, I headed out in a long sleeved flannel shirt and jeans and wore gardening gloves. I felt as though I was suited for battle, bucket in one hand and knife or scissors in the other.

The advantageous part about the entire experience was the reward: one of my mom's fried okra sandwiches. Yes, indeed, there's nothing like the aroma of the fruit of your labor wafting into your nostrils from your mom's large, heavy skillet. And there's nothing like enjoying that fried delicacy between two slices of white bread with thinly sliced fresh onions and tomatoes. I was in heaven.

When you're a kid, you're hardly aware of the reasons, the whys, or hows, or of the what for's. You simply live your life one day at a time, as though in a slow motion picture, mostly without sound, wishing you didn't have to help with the gardening. While many of my friends were spending their summers working on their tans, being lathered in Copper-Tone oil as they lounged about the pool while wearing the latest teeny-weeny polka dot bikinis, you guessed it . . . I was gardening.

Ironiclly, being the daughter of a naturalist, I spent my summers sweltering in the sun, living my summers out working in the fresh soil, breathing in the clean air, taking on the appearance of a zebra, and sporting what my rancher husband calls a farmer's tan. I was striped from head to toe.

Anyway, it wasn't until I became a chef much later in my life, that I began to value some of the treasures I was handed, one of them being the love for fresh food. I also valued the knowledge of gardening I learned along the way.

During a long season of confusion and what I'll call a misunderstood darkness, I had an epiphany: all seeds start in the dark, lonely ground. In that time, buried inside the earth, that single, insignificant, small seed begins to sprout and form roots. As the roots grow, they spread out and go down deep inside the earth to give them a foundation.

Now, without a solid healthy root system, the plant will never survive Mother Natures wind, heavy rain, extreme heat, and drought. It will never be able to absorb nutrients, produce blooms, or bear fruit. It is the root that is the support for the plant in every way. And it is only in seclusion that the roots are developed.

Bam! This revelation blew me away. That thing I had known for so many years began to make sense.

────── THE ESPRESSO FACTOR ──────

If we are to grow strong. If we are to bloom. If, indeed, we are ever to produce fruit and fulfill our destiny, we must first experience the darkness. Growth is in the darkness. It's in the shadows that we mature. It's in the murky night seasons of life that we develop.

It's easy to curse the dark times, those times we feel unnoticed, rejected, and barren. Those are the times we see nothing. It is in the fruitless times that we may experience nothing but confusion and perturbation.

The darkness is sorely misunderstood, but it is simply part of life. Instead of being afraid of the dark, we should relish in it, knowing we're going to be fabulous when the sun hits our face.

Can you relate? Ever been in a dark season? Did you curse it or embrace it? Did you allow the darkness to stretch your faith or did you throw temper tantrums?

What did you learn while in the dark?

My prayer for you is that you learn to trust the process even when you find yourself in the dark. The darkness is simply part of the journey.

Don't be afraid of the dark.

I don't know about you, but I ain't afraid of no ghost.

I Love Grey Poupon

You can't judge a tree by the size of its seed.

The mustard seed is one of the smallest in the world, yet when a mustard tree is full grown, it can stretch up to twenty feet in the air, spreading out to the same width.

It has many essential uses, much more than as a condiment for our American favorite, the cheeseburger. The mustard seed is a mere two millimeters in size, yet inside its insignificant-appearing shell is much strength. Much power. Much potential.

With buying vintage property comes a lot of hard work; the latest purchase was no exception. There was much over-growth to be cleared: volunteer plants had to be pulled out, weeds needed killed and dead branches hauled off. Amongst all this futile growth, stand two nearly one-hundred-year-old mulberry trees. They've seen much; they've survived much. Yet they continue to shade and protect and wave honorably in the breeze.

As I toiled and sweat in temperatures pushing one hundred degrees, I couldn't help but ponder on the tenacity of these trees not only to persevere but to multiply. They did not wallow in their circumstances but allowed their roots to reach deeper into the earth, giving them a sturdier foundation which helped them endure the storms and droughts that most definitely come with living.

Sometimes I feel as minuscule as a mustard seed: insignificant and meager. And then I am reminded of the potential this seed holds in its adult stages of life. I look up toward the vast sky at my one-hundred-year-old mulberry trees and see their steadfast beauty. Both trees have their purpose. Both trees started out as what seemed as insignificant seeds. And yet, they live out their purpose not questioning their slight, humble beginnings but simply doing what they were designed to do.

We cannot judge our lives, our potential, our purpose by our small beginnings. We should not wish for a grand inception but trust and believe that humble beginnings can and will grow into something opulent and glorious. If only we persevere.

The mustard tree does not despise its tiny self when tossed into the dark, damp earth because it believes in its destiny and it simply allows itself grace to grow. The mulberry trees did not fret when the winds came; they prepared for the storm.

I want to be like the mustard seed. And when I see myself as small, I must remind myself not to look at my size, but at my potential. When storms come—as they have and will again—I must reflect on my mulberry trees, allow my roots to grow deeper into the strong foundation that has been around since before the beginning of time—God and His grace.

I want to be like the tree that is planted by the rivers of living water. Not only surviving but flourishing, and multiplying and giving back.

——— THE ESPRESSO FACTOR ———

One should not look at the size of the seed but at the destiny the small seed holds.

Are you okay with a small beginning? If not, what is it about a small beginning you don't like?

Are you lazy and want to skip a few steps, or are you are you embarrassed because you fear other people's opinions?

Do you fear you won't succeed if you don't reach your goal in record time? Be honest with yourself.

The journey is not about becoming an overnight success. It's about living and growing and learning.

Chillax Chicas, you're gonna get there.

Consider the trees; they hold the key.

One Lonely Seed

---

*The weeds and the wildflowers can all look the
same. It's not up to us to decide.*

There was a seed. One. Lonely. Seed. Hiding, existing, en-
during the fear it had convinced itself it was betrothed
to. Fully omitting the fact there was no real evidence proving
a dowry had been paid. Nonetheless, it lingered safely nestled
deep in a dark nook, a sterile womb. It gave no thought to the
potential or opportunities that lie dormant inside the marrow of
its hard-shelled exterior.

Convinced it was only a weed and destined simply to
silently occupy space, the seed was not content but accepted
what seemed to be its plight; this was all life had to offer. Never
entertaining the fact that maybe, just maybe, it existed for such
a time as this.

* * *

One Saturday morning after a lengthy, entertaining breakfast at a local diner with our kids, and grandkids, we met back at my café for an iced espresso. While sipping our icy drinks and discussing the landscaping in our backyards, I smiled at the new seedlings peeping their little green faces up through the damp earth, remembering how barren, rocky, and weedy the lot was when we first moved in. Except for one lonely miniature sunflower.

It stood proudly amidst all that seemed forlorn and forgotten. It was all alone, but there it stood. I recall Poppa Bear tenderly transplanting it to a more desirable spot, where he watered it, tended to it, and nurtured it.

It grew that summer and made seed that fall. Come spring the seeds that had fallen from that single tiny bloom germinated, and the backyard soon became a wildflower paradise.

Yellow blooms lined our fence, extending over into the alley, making even an eyesore lovely. There was beauty galore because one tiny seed had the tenacity to fight through the rocks and stretch forth beyond the hard crusty soil.

It refused to give up but chose to flourish and become exactly what it was created to be: a beautiful flower to adorn our backyard, provide nectar for the bees, and shelter for the newly born rabbits we had encountered. Come autumn, their seeds would become nourishment for the sparrows.

Oh, yes, all that from one small insignificant seed deciding to grow and live and thrive, even against all odds. Thank goodness for the keen eye and sensitivity of Poppa Bear who did the rescuing.

I want to be just like that wildflower, persevering when the sandburs try to choke me out, laughing in the face of fear, being determined to make my destiny count against all obstacles. Yes, against all odds.

As I contemplate this seed, that oh so tiny embryo, I see a parable, a story not unlike ours, born free of fear. We are born with an unlimited potential to do the phenomenal, the enchanting, the lovely. All of us have the capability to transform our surroundings with hope and worthiness, and excellence. Each of us are born with our own wow factor. Yet, too often we allow the crusty, frightful, hideous times of drought to hold our true qualifications captive in the womb. We sit by and give up and bit by bit, little pieces of us die until we've become part of an unsightly landscape, feeling barren and hopeless, never really living, only existing.

The fact is, life really is going to be a little rocky at times. The truth is, there's gonna be a drought, whether it be financially, physically, or even spiritually, at some point in our life.

News flash: some time or another, we're all gonna need a little TLC. There's going to come a time we feel like a weed or even be mistaken for one. The question is, will we allow fear to overcome us or will we be like the wild sunflower that pushed through the sandburs and stones, hanging on through the drought, never losing hope until a rescuer comes?

THE ESPRESSO FACTOR

Before I lay my pen down and come to the end of this simple little anecdote, I feel the need to share something about myself. Many years ago, when man-made religious rules governed my life, I judged something or someone I clearly was not in a position to judge.

And as I stood in all my self-righteousness, bringing my own interpretation into a scenario, deep within me came a resounding voice: "how dare you judge; for you do not have the ability to arbitrate nor to differentiate between true weeds and wildflowers."

At that moment I knew I had been given a new kind of perception. I had been granted the opportunity to view life through a different lens. I traded in judgement for clemency and now, I have no doubt whatsoever that there really is greatness: a rare beauty and treasured grace inside us all. It is all there. Everything we need. We just have to embrace it.

And I am certain of this very thing: we were all made for such a time as this.

Please, take the time to write down some dream seeds you've allowed to lay dormant. You know, the ones you thought were weeds.

What's your wow factor? Write it down. Nurture it, and watch it transform your entire surroundings.

Because, sometimes we only think we see weeds.

6

DON'T SWEAT THE POO, SIMPLY ENJOY THE RIDE

Dog Strollers,
Scabbed Knees, and Poo

Laughter comes easy when we hit a triple.
It comes in handy when we bite the dust.

Neil (a.k.a. Poppa Bear), is a left-brain thinker. He is not a multi-tasker. He does not have conversations with himself, in his head—ever. And he always, I mean *always* weighs the pros against the cons. I am the complete opposite.

I like to describe him as a dial-up model. Me? Well, I am 5G. I walk fast. I talk fast. I have a continual monologue running in my head day and night and make decisions at the drop of a hat.

Poppa Bear likes practicality and everything must make sense in his head and on paper before any decision is made. Every *T* has to be crossed and all the *I*s dotted.

I follow my gut. I am the mover and shaker.

He is the foundation stabilizer. You know those infrastructure repair guys that fix the foundation of your house if it cracks or sags or leans? He's that guy in my life.

Now, don't get me wrong. Poppa Bear is not a slow learner, nor is he inadequate in the IQ realm. He's one of the smartest men you will ever meet. He simply is an analyzer. High IQ people do that you know. And I say, who has time to analyze? Just dive right in.

Case in point: one not-so-extraordinary day I was bebopping around the café making lattes, smoothies, and cookies. I was answering the phone, taking orders, and trotting them out to the curb. Life was good.

I was rocking it as I bounced my way into the utility closet with a song on my lips and thankfulness in my heart. I reached up high to grab a sleeve of take-out lids, twirled around, and headed back to the kitchen. People were waiting on their orders and time was of the essence.

Poppa Bear was at the stove, slowly but steadily making himself an omelet.

I will admit, I have too much stuff in my utility closet. One of those things that should have never been placed in there was Dior's pink dog stroller. It was folded up and leaning against the wall. I had good intentions of putting it in its proper place at day's end but figured it was fine for now. And it was fine . . . until it wasn't.

Like I was saying, I reached up to grab a sleeve of take-out lids, swung around, caught the stroller with my toe, which caused a domino effect. The stroller rolled out into the middle of the small room, my brick red Birkenstock mule went flying, and in slow motion I sailed, with no grace whatsoever, over the top of the stroller, coming down on my left knee and shoulder. To finish off the fiasco, I slid across the floor as if I were sliding onto home base in the World Series. And then I screamed.

Poppa Bear froze. I could see him through the small doorway, standing, spatula in one hand and a blank look on his face. I could tell the wheels were turning: *Do I continue to cook the omelet? Will the omelet be ruined if I take it off the burner before it's cooked? Where's the burner? And what do I do with this spatula I have in my hand?*

I screamed again, and in his usual steady stride he arrived at my side, lifted me up from the floor, gave me a hug, asked if I was hurt, and then proceeded to tell me how Dior's stroller did not belong in the utility closet in the first place.

Is there a lesson here?

Don't pile stuff in your utility closet that doesn't belong there?

Don't wear mules on really busy days?

Don't try to multitask at high speed?

Or maybe it's simply: even on the very best sunshiny days poo can happen.

We can feel discombobulated and out of sorts. We can fall flat on our faces. We can get scuffed and bruised and cry out at high decimals. But one truth remains: we all have our own World Series in which to play.

Sometimes life comes at us with a flawless pitch. It executes with ideal timing, the right speed and perfect command, setting us up for a grand slam home run. But most days it is a grounder here, a double there, a few singles, and if we're lucky, we just might get to steal home a time or two.

What I have learned by watching my firstborn grandson through many years of little league, high school and then college baseball is that there will always be an abundance of strikes along the way. The exciting news is, at the end of the day, it's the final score that counts.

I say when the poo shows up, it's more than okay to take a short time to nurse our wounds. But then comes the moment to make the choice: do we jump up, dust ourselves off, laugh at ourselves and continue, or do we choose to mope off the field, hang up our cleats, and make excuses for why we don't suit up and get back in the game?

I choose to laugh. Laughter is much more fun. Besides, on this one particular day, I had customers waiting at the curb for their iced coffees, so I most definitely found the laughter—after the tears, of course.

But I laughed because laughter is medicine for the soul.

THE ESPRESSO FACTOR

The strikeouts will come.

"Put me in coach, I'm ready to play . . . today." This was one of my favorite songs played between innings as I watched the pitchers warm up their fastball and the batters take practice swings. I watched my Kade play for several years. He always had a look of determination on his face as he stepped up to the batter's box. As the opposing team chided, "Swing batter, batter swing," he honed in on his target.

Many times in his baseball career, we'd hear an exploding crack as the ball flew high in the sky and over the fence, giving him an easy trot around the bases and over home plate.

I have sat through games, however, where no matter how determined he was, he'd get three strikes in a row and be out; not out of the entire game, of course, just out of that inning.

When his time came to bat again, he would approach the batter's box with every bit of perseverance and passion as before. Playing with fortitude, he knew what his potential was.

When we find ourselves right smack dab in the middle of a strikeout, it's easy to coddle our wounds, feel sorry for ourselves, and make excuses.

What if Kade would have pleaded with the coach to bench him after a tough inning? He never would have gotten those grand slams. And his baseball career would have ended prematurely.

What do you do when you find yourself flailing about, hitting strikes, and feeling as if you've landed face down in the dirt?

No, seriously? What have you done in the past? If you benched yourself, did you stay in the dug out? Or did you put your cleats back on and walk proudly up to the batters box?

If you are still in the dugout, what or who is keeping you there?

What are you afraid of?

Now, get up, suit up and be the star player in your own World Series.

A Quick Run to the Grocer

But then the burglar alarm sounded.

I was in the middle of prepping for the book signing event I was hosting for some friends from Dallas. I had no time to tarry. I knew the store would be packed with people stopping by on their way home from work to grab dinner items, but it would be what it would be, and I'd do my best to hurry things along.

With paid-for items piled in my cart, I fled the store with fervor to get back to the café and continue my prep work. The day's temp had reached a high of only thirty-two degrees. It was a bit breezy, so I wasted no time walking to the far end of row 5 of the parking lot.

I always park on row 5. It keeps me from wondering the concrete labyrinth, pushing my cart around looking like a lost bag lady. It's just better that way. It saves me from frustration, embarrassment, and lost time when I am in a hurry, when my mind is in go mode and I flee from my Jeep never looking around to where I might have landed, which is most days. Yes indeed, it is always row 5 for me.

I had actually made good time and was in and out of the grocery store with ease, considering the crowd. With my Jeep fob in my backpack, I pulled at the handle to open the door. I pulled the handle a second time; the door remained locked.

Digging to the bottom of the black hole I call my backpack, I grabbed the fob and pushed unlock. Nada. I clicked again and again, and still nothing happened.

I looked around twice to double check, making sure I wasn't mistaken on who's Jeep I was trying to gain entry. Go ahead and laugh, because it is true, I have made this gaffe before; but yes, both times it was confirmed that this vehicle was mine.

Out of options, I took a wild guess that maybe the fob battery had died. There I was, stuck in the freezing wintery air, so I called Poppa Bear asking for advice. He told me about the emergency key inside the fob. Who knew? I removed the key and unlocked the door. I thought I was home free until the alarm began to sound. No matter how I tried to silence the obnoxious noise, it just keep going.

There is one major advantage to living in a small town; it takes only a few minutes to go from location A to location B. The alarm continued to sound as I sat inside the screaming Jeep until my knight in shining armor showed up with the extra fob in hand.

The plight had been resolved and all was well.

THE ESPRESSO FACTOR

Lesson for the day: as we slide into new adventures, laugh out loud.

It's a wise woman who can remember to laugh when she is huddling from the cold, inside a Jeep, in the middle of a grocer's parking lot with the car alarm screaming loud enough to wake the dead. It's a wiser one who can laugh when her journey looks as if it has been derailed and the train to Smoothville has been delayed.

Are you being detained by situations and obstacles over which you have no control? Remind yourself how temporal most obstacles are as you write, placing yourself in the starring role, a one-page sitcom of your latest fiasco. Now laugh out loud as you read it back to yourself.

Believe me, it'll put everything in perspective and makes for a brighter day.

Snafus never last long, but women who can laugh at them do.

Life Is More than a Five-and-Dime Mechanical Pony

Be fearless like a tot.
It's the way life was intended.

I was raised riding horses. It was more natural for me to ride a horse than to ride a bike. Day in, day out, I was riding. From a tot until I was well into adulthood, I rode nearly every day. It was my freedom space.

Sparky had been my dad's gelding from a colt. He was a sorrel that stretched up to seventeen hands in height. He was a cowboy's horse. Raised out on the pastureland among the cattle, he was used to being ridden through sagebrush, down into small canyons, and over rough terrain.

He was as gentle on most days as anyone could imagine, yet he could spook easily if the atmosphere around him suddenly became flustered.

I can clearly remember the day. I am always astonished at the things that are forever burned in our memory. I have no answer for that, but I do know I can still picture my surroundings on this memorable day. I was young, like really little, no older than four years of age. It was back when every family had a clothesline, a heavy wire that was strung ten to fifteen feet across the yard, connected to fence posts that were placed in the ground and reached six feet in the air. This was an era when most moms took pride in hanging newly washed laundry out in the fresh clean air with wooden clothes pins to dry. My mom was no exception.

This day was not laundry day. It was the day I got to ride Sparky. He was bridled, saddled, and ready to go. I was giddy about the way everything had played itself out. It was a peaceful day in our backyard, in Mooreland, Oklahoma. I sat upon a well-worn saddle that swallowed me up, and I giggled. I had the power; I held the reins. And I was pleased as punch to sit quietly upon this oversized pony, until . . . he bolted.

I had no choice but to follow and hang on tight. Just as quickly as I had ricocheted forward, we came to a halt. There I was lying backward, flat against the saddle, chin hooked with the clothesline. And Sparky, as if suddenly remembering he carried precious cargo, stood perfectly still.

All is well that ends well. For the rest of the day, I allowed my daddy to be in control of the reins

There's only been one time I've been pinned to the saddle by a clothesline, but more than once, I have believed myself to be in control. There have been more times than I can count, that I have thought I was big enough, smart enough, powerful enough to fly solo. You know, handle my own reins. Be in charge. And when that happens, my life projectiles forward. I find I am not at all in control. And by some unforeseen miracle, to save me from myself, life comes to a complete standstill.

Some days I feel like that small, curly headed girl. I believe that simply holding the reins of something bigger and more powerful than myself is all I need to put me in charge and make me capable. I can sit straight in the saddle, gripping the leather straps of the harness, but my naivete can put me in the danger zone. I am then forced to come to a standstill or take a fierce tumble.

Other days, life is like the cheap mechanical horse perched in concrete in front of the local five and dime my mom would allow me to ride, for a nickel.

I loved riding that stay-in-place pony. It was a little treat given to me from my mother whenever we shopped the TG&Y variety store. It was safe. If it ever looked as if it were out of control, all you had to do was unplug it.

In reality, life is the sorrel gelding Sparky; when we least expect it, it bolts, and we realize it can be much harder to handle than we were willing to admit. The standstills may simply be there to help us understand that we really can't do it alone. The standstills just may be our saving grace.

Our personalized journey is about discovering our strengths, acknowledging our weaknesses, and admitting we could use some guidance. As we grow; as we mature, we look around and see we might have been a little too big for our own britches, or maybe the saddle. Needing help but not wanting it, we yearn to run when we can barely walk. We want to fly but haven't even boarded the plane.

But then there is God's grace: always there wanting to teach, watching over us, always faithful and willing to take the reins. When we find ourselves pinned down by our mishaps, God steps in and does what He does best: He rescues us.

He never pushes or invades; he stands beside us, quietly waiting for us to ask Him to take the reins.

I suppose there was a time in my life that I had to learn to trust that He really does do what he says He'll do. What a comfort to know He is always willing to take charge of the reins, be my help when I am in need and my encourager when I am tempted to sit in the shadows allowing a few bumpy days to keep me from riding my own Sparky.

—— **THE ESPRESSO FACTOR** ——

We weren't designed to have a "play it safe" mentality. We were created to live life out loud. Our Creator wants us to sit high in our saddle, hold on tight, and allow Him to take the lead rope. I've tried it both ways; I've played it safe and

I've lived out loud. I happen to like living with wonder and adventure much better.

When I put God in charge, the adventure and wonder are beyond anything I can imagine or ask for. If you happen to find yourself entangled, He'll help you sort through the unforeseen snafus, and sit you upright with absolutely no lectures or condemnation.

The cool thing is, He allows for mistakes. In fact, He welcomes our gaffs and silliness and faux pas. They give Him a chance to do what He does best: rescue us. For His grace is sufficient. It is more than enough to cover every single weakness we have.

Do you play it safe or are you a "give me the reins and let me ride" kinda girl? We all have our "play it safe" zones. Sometimes it's wise to have them; sometimes they are a deterrent.

Write about your safe zones, your own runaway horse or what you have learned about the standstills. Please, stay away from the woulda, coulda, shouldas. Life isn't about wishing we had done something different; it's about learning and growing and becoming wiser.

Life is a rodeo. What are you waiting for? Saddle up and ride.

7

INVEST IN THE RIGHT GEAR

The Espresso Factor

Life Can Be a Rodeo

Be sure ya invest in the right gear.

I'm from cowboy country. You know, the land where ten-gal-lon hats, oversized belt buckles, and Wrangler jeans rule. I've been to my share of rodeos and have seen my share of bronc riding, calf roping, bulldogging, and barrel racing. It's all exciting, but the bull riding event is definitely my favorite.

If you are a rodeo fan, you know that rodeo people are some of the most fervid people on the planet.

One of the most majestic, patriotic sights you will ever see is at the beginning of the event when a skydiver jumps out of an airplane holding the American flag. As he drops through the air, the flag waves in the breeze and God Bless America plays loud and proud over the speakers.

Boy Scouts plant themselves inside the perfectly graded dirt floor arena ready to go into action. Their job is to catch the flag before it hits the ground. They always complete their task well, fold it properly and walk respectfully out of the ring.

I invariably get a lump in my throat as I stand, hand over my heart, at the grandeur of it all.

I've been attending rodeos since I could barely walk. My mom always made sure my sisters and I were dressed in real cowgirl style, complete with red cowboy boots. Oh gosh, how I loved my red boots. I still love red boots, and truth be known, I have several pair in my closet. I simply can't help myself.

It's a well-known fact that real cowgirls and cowboys wear cowboy boots. I've never rodeoed myself, but I do know as of to date, I have yet to see a bull rider ride out his 8 seconds in flip-flops. I have yet to see my rancher husband feed cattle in a pair of TOMS. I have never seen my dad check on calving heifers in a pair of canvas Converse.

Cowboys know their boots. They understand that a good pair is going to cost them some bank. They also understand that a well-made pair is an investment they can't afford to scrimp on. They know the job that lies ahead may be a tough one, and having the right equipment (spurs, ropes, leather gloves, pliers, baling wire, and yes, a great pair of boots) makes the day go smoother.

In my café, I have my own equipment: chef knives, cutting boards, pucks, espresso tampers, blenders, and a plethora of pitchers, bowls, measuring spoons, and mixers. These all are must haves when one owns a coffee shop.

The equipment one uses on the job is extremely important, but my real equipment, the equipment that gets me through the day, that helps keep a hop in my step, hope in my heart, and a smile on my face is my belief system.

I believe that all things are possible and that the sun will shine tomorrow even if it's raining today. I believe that I have a purpose, and that I was born for such a time as this. I have no doubt that God will get me where I need to go if only I stay chill and allow Him to take the lead.

Our equipment can either work for us or against us. Our belief system has the power to create joy and peace, confidence and courage, or make our life's journey a rocky, desolate, dry one. It will either be the springboard we need to help us succeed or be the lariat that corrals us.

THE ESPRESSO FACTOR

Our journey requires us to have the right equipment. Just like the bull riders, cattle ranchers and chefs. In our occupation, it's the tools we choose that make the job easier and more efficient.

So if the right physical tools are essential, why shouldn't our emotional and spiritual tools be just as important?

Are you deficient in hope?

Are you fighting depression, fear, or discouragement?

Have you given up on the fact that you have a purpose and a destiny?

What paradigm shift needs to happen in order for you to regain hope?

Maybe you've invested in the wrong equipment, the wrong kind of thinking or perspective. Now think about it for a moment. Maybe it's time to upgrade.

Make a list of the obsolete "tools" you've been hanging on to. Beside each outdated "tool," write down what you're going to replace each thought, action, or belief system with. For example: you may be thinking, "I'm an average Pollyanna, how could I have an influential purpose in life?" Trade it in for, "I choose to believe that I was born for such a time as this."

Do me a favor, better yet, do yourself one. Meditate on the new tools every day for at least a week. I am willing to bet you're going to see a huge change. Now, don't stop. Continue using them and forge ahead.

It's time to cowgirl up.

Muddy Boots and All

If the mountain refuses to move, climb it.

After wheeling Poppa Bear into the operating room for a minimally invasive stent surgery the doctors discovered he needed a quintuple bypass. Poppa Bear himself didn't have a clue. He was drugged, and it was left up to me to cross this slippery slope on my own.

I was in shock. I had expected one thing, but learned quickly that things were not as they seemed.

Times like these—grandiose moments. times of pandemonium, islands of both solitude and celebrations, momentary lush rain forests giving way to crusty, dry deserts, babies being born, and sometimes dying——cause us to stop and meditate on life, always bringing us to the end, the climax, the finale of something brilliant or devastating. When we come face to face with the end however, not unlike a Jason Bourne movie, we are never certain what the next mission will be.

I am a coffee shop owner. I eat, sleep and breathe coffee. When the invitation came from my roaster to join his team on a sourcing trip, the answer was an easy one and I quickly said, "I'm in". A few months later, I was hiking my way up the mountains into the coffee fields of Haiti for the very first time. The view of creation from the summit will forever resound in my soul. The breathtaking panorama of the cosmos reverberates still in my memory.

It was as lush as a rainforest, but the unmarked trails were slippery with overgrowth concealing a sloppy, precarious, muddy mess, making for unreliable footing. Despite my careful maneuvering I lost my footing and came crashing down on all fours, looking very undignified in front of my millennial peers.

I was the only grandmum of the group, and not wanting to appear old, I popped up with damaged pride intact. I may have been filled with embarrassment, but I also found tenacity and determination.

As I continued on the upward journey towards my destination, I learned there was a technique to climbing slippery slopes. I discovered if I would dig my heels in first while stepping, I could set my foundation before I took my next step towards the top.

I learned there was a technique to climbing slippery slopes, and as I progressed up the mountain, the journey became easier, and the view more beautiful. It was surreal. It was magnificent. At the top, the words would not come but the tears that flowed down my face said it all.

After the trek was over and we had reached the bottom once again, my once clean and brilliantly polished boots were now caked with gray mud, scratched and gouged from the rough foliage, and sported the appearance of abuse. However, giving them a second glance, I noticed not misuse but adventure and engagement and purpose. I thought, *Wow! What if, after falling, looking a bit weak and silly, and, yes old, I had given up? What if I had succumbed to frustration, fear, and mortification when landing belly down in the mud?*

What if I had chosen to end my journey there? What if I had waited, sitting on a tree stump, half way up the mountainside while the rest of my troop had persevered? What if I had sat my butt down and, like a stubborn mule, refused to move because of the rough terrain?

Without a doubt I can tell you how the story would have ended. I would have missed out on one of the most magnificent, thrilling experiences I've ever had. And my muddy boots wouldn't have had an adventure story to tell.

——— THE ESPRESSO FACTOR ———

Without sounding too cliché, life can be messy. At any given time, it can be filled with mud, embarrassment, failures, and mishaps. Without adversity and ensuing tenacity, one never reaches the top of the mountain.

Without digging our heels in, our odyssey is cut short, and we never experience the true beauty at the top. Without going through the mud and rough spots, we never truly learn just how brave we can be.

The most grandeur thing about it all is, yes, we may get muddy and crusty and scraped up, but just like my boots, with a little cleaning up; with a little polishing, buffing, and a spit and shine; we reveal a unique patina that exposes our true grit.

That patina shows we have explored and persisted not simply existed. It shows we've dared to expose our weaknesses. And just like my boots, we can know we have fulfilled our purpose; we didn't cower or give up, nor did we hide in safety's shadows. We dared to trample over obstacles and climb mountains we've never climbed. And we have won.

While spending several days sitting in hospital waiting rooms while Poppa Bear recovered from his surgery, I spent an exuberant number of hours people watching and drinking gallons of bitter, burnt coffee from the visitors lobby.

Sitting next to others, I was exposed to stories that no doubt would have less than a happy ending, but with each story came emotions tying me to other families in anguished situations.

I'm in the hospitality business, so of course I felt my heart searching for ways to comfort the hurting, the isolated, the heavy hearted, the best way I knew how. The only sane thing I knew to do was surprise them with the good stuff: lattes and cookies from the coffee shop down the street.

So I did just that. I loaded up the Jeep with as much java and cookies as I could carry and began passing them out in the waiting room. This brought smiles to many hurting faces; it gave me peace, made me feel useful and delivered a bit of normalcy to my own stressful day.

There was no doubt we were all, that day, trying to find our footing in uncharted terrain, digging our heels in, figuring out how to build the foundation to get to the top of our own mountain.

Treating people to coffee and cookies helped me build my foundation. Lending kindness, giving hugs and being an encouragement even as I felt my own emotions being taken under siege, kept me focused on the mountaintop not the muddy, slippery slope. I was determined to win.

The moral to the story? Don't worry so much about the mud, but look for ways to get yourself to the top of your mountain.

Are you stuck in the mud? Have you fallen and refuse to get up? Are you feeling sorry for yourself because the mountain won't move?

What happened to make you lose your faith? Lose your footing?

Figure out what you must do to help build a firmer foundation while climbing to the top. Have you invested in the right gear; faith, hope, love, determination?

What are you waiting for? Find your footing and climb that mountain.

What's in Your Bucket?

Don't buy the bucket. There are no pigs to be fed.

Somewhere, at some moment in time, most of us have been sold a bill of nonessential goods, a complete library of propaganda, a bucketful of slop, if you will. When our journey goes rogue, this propaganda becomes like a resounding gong, taunting us with mindless garbage.

In order for us to do our part and be a responsible administrator of our own epic journey, we believe we must worry, stew, lose sleep, overeat, and experience anxiety, among other things. And, of course, we certainly aren't opposed to adding a few bitchy days in for good measure.

We make ourselves a sickly mess until things line up with our agenda once again, or we compromise and settle or maybe even manipulate the situation in order for us to arrive at a resolution.

Never mind that the resolution reached may be less than the best for us. Or worse, it may usher in weightier problems later on. Let's be real, most times we are stoked to have gotten our way. We inhale a deep breath, give a sigh of relief, wipe the sweat from our brow, and continue on our merry way. Dilemma solved, right?

What a visual; a slop bucket. I haven't thought about a slop bucket since I was a young girl. That word takes me back to the farm and my visits with my Grandpa and Grandma K. They always had a slop bucket setting on the floor next to the kitchen sink. This was pre-garbage disposal days, and the five-gallon, galvanized bucket served as a receptacle for the food particles left on the plates, the crumbs from the table cloth, bits left in the pots and pans, and leftover glasses of milk.

As a girl, I guess I never really thought much about the reasoning behind having a bucket for such a purpose. I suspect now, as I look back, their plumbing probably wasn't too good plus the left over sludge was used to feed the pigs, explaining the old adage, "slop the hogs."

Anyway, after a couple of days' worth of food scraps and waste—vegetable peels, breadcrumbs, old grease, and leftover gravy—all mixed into a rotting soup, this bucket was, to say the least, a putrid, odiferous mess.

Some days are simply for pondering and reflecting. I have grown to respect these days as usually an epiphany comes. After making its way into my soul and eventually into my head, it takes up residency in my heart. "Enjoy where you are on the way to where you are going." This old, familiar phrase resonates within and peace follows. I have heard this quote too many times to count, but the truth finally flickers through the garbage and a patina as bright as a rainbow bedazzles me.

There are just some situations I cannot control or fix, whether they be social, relational, or pertaining to my business. Sometimes, even after doing all I can to fix issues and problems and snafus, I just have to take a step back, throw our hands in the air, and stand and wait.

Standing, waiting, resting, is not an easy task for me to accomplish. I'm a doer, a dreamer, a fixer, and a motivator. But unmistakably there are times when I have to be real with myself and admit that motivators and cheerleaders are not life gurus nor do they have the ability to revise everything broken or askew.

I for one, have trekked this path before, with hiking boots knotted tightly, and a backpack loaded with my chosen essentials. I have positioned myself at the foot of the same darn mountain, gazing up at an overwhelming elevation to be climbed, once again. I am rediscovering I am not a super hero. I never will be, as neither will you. Just 100 percent human.

—— THE ESPRESSO FACTOR ——

Life is a learning curve, really. Some days you get it right, and others, well, that brings us to God's grace. Always waiting, always near, ready in an instant to do what we, ourselves cannot do. Forever on standby, listening for the slightest bit of invitation to be the arbitrator of all things big and small.

We cannot control a large number of life's calamities, but we can trust grace. We can turn the radio up loud, sing a happy song, laugh intensely, read a good book, do a kind act for a neighbor, and never, ever find it necessary to buy a five-gallon galvanized bucket in which to stash all our worries, despairs, concerns, and worldly sorrows.

It only takes a brief time of harboring such rubbish that our soul becomes the slop bucket, and we begin to reek of sourness, live in pain and anxiety, and become moldy and rancid. And soon, the newly purchased buckets begin to hinder us from enjoying the trip. They begin to rob us of the joy of the actual journey. It's not about the perfection of the journey; it's about the thrills and the grins and the giggles we have on the excursion itself.

As I continue to cherish my future and wait for answers concerning my promenade on life's boardwalk, I want to encourage you to ignore the slop bucket and choose the joy in this present moment, leaving tomorrow to sort itself out.

For I know if given a chance all things will work together for your benefit.

Do you rely on God to handle your garbage or are you allowing your soul to be the slop bucket?

Are you storing all the unwanted trash—anger, offenses, fear, timidity, etc.—in the new bucket, hoping no one will notice?

The thing is, just like my grandparent's bucket, eventually it's going to stink.

Write down all the good things that are happening in your life. Read it out loud to yourself. Faith and healing and freedom come from hearing the good news.

Let the trash you've been hoarding fall to the wayside. Allow God's grace to help you deal with it.

And don't buy the bucket. There aren't any pigs to feed.

Don't Forget to Flush

The unused matter can be toxic.

And the volcano erupted. Full force. The pressure had been building. The temperature was rising; underneath the surface, tension was surging. No one could stop it.

Toxic gases were forming. It was hot, ugly, vile, and dangerous if you were caught standing in its way. It never was a respecter of persons, and when the pressure reached its limits, it erupted.

I think most of us understand that our bodies were designed to need nutrition, right? We become hungry and need fuel, so we eat.

It is up to us to eat the nutritious, healthy stuff. We can choose fruits, veggies, whole grains, and, yes, a New York strip, grilled to a perfect medium, once in a while. That would be a nutritional lifestyle.

Our bodies extract the nutrients and then, as we say, Mother Nature calls, and we release the toxins in the bathroom.

Please know I really am trying my best to be as refined with my words as possible, so bear with me here. It's nature's way. We all do it. Some are just more comfortable with the topic than others.

In fact, if I have an upset stomach, Poppa Bear asks, "Have you pooped today? If my sinuses are acting up, "do you need to poop?" And, if I've had an exhausting day, you guessed it, "Did you take time to poop?"

If we choose healthy, clean, pure foods, the process is much less toxic and wallpaper-peeling than if we have been through the fast food drive-through too many times in one week. Remember, scientifically we release the leftovers, the part of our food our bodies cannot use. The junkier the food, the more vile the gasses and leftover solids we release. And so it goes with our soul. Whatever we have stored away in our heart, whatever we have ingested and dwelled upon in our minds, the mouth will eventually speak.

If fear dwells in our soul, we will speak words of dread and doubt. If hate has taken up residence, a voice of poisonous venom will flow. If rejection is allowed to become a tenant, anger will spew. Greed and self-centeredness will hoard in stressful times; bitterness will spew resentment; if we are depressed, our emotions will bleed out gloom, doom, agony, and despair.

The good news is, if we've been diligent to watch what we feed our soul, there will be no ugly smelly gases building up. Where there is hope, there will be kindness and charity.

Where there is faith, happiness, peace, and gratitude will triumph.

Just like the volcano, when the temperature reaches its limits, when the pressure is on in hard times, something from within us is going to come out. It's a given. It's the human way.

—— THE ESPRESSO FACTOR ——

In this era in which we are living, it seems we all are under siege. And I stand in the shadows observing people's retort to it all: hateful rants on social media, impatience at the grocer, disrespect towards the servers in the restaurants. So much anger, hoarding, doomsday attitudes, and fear.

It is a battlefield of landmines waiting to explode with each step we take. And one explosion leads to another.

It is a breath of fresh air when I run across someone who exudes peace that bypasses all understanding, who speaks hope instead of fear, reacts with apathy not impatience, and can look calamity in the eye and laugh. Indeed, it is a rare thing these days.

And like a hotheaded volcano, our society is erupting. The evidence is everywhere I turn.

It's inevitable. What's inside us is going to come out.

It's examination time. What's tucked away in your heart? What kind of soul food have you been feeding on? Is it time to change your diet?

How toxic is your spew? Because if it doesn't bring hope, if it's not love, joy, and peace, please don't forget to flush.

8

FIND YOUR MOXIE

The Espresso Factor

Will I Ever Outgrow
My Terrible Twos?

*Though I strive to do good, I always continue to
be weak in some areas, and, alas,
I disappoint myself.*

There are times in life when we think we have begun to mature, times we think we are forever done with pettiness and then something happens, and we find we are nothing more than a toddler still making her way through the terrible twos.

Jace is a curly-headed, blued-eyed toddler who frequents my café once or twice a week with his mom. He has been a customer from the womb, learning my voice and experiencing my signature iced coffees before he ever took his first breath. *Rita* was one of his first words he learned to say.

This little guy's visits never fail to be entertaining and bring a smile to my face. One morning while standing at the espresso machine I looked up to see a motorized, toddler size racecar coming through my red French door. He came rolling in, face beaming.

"I want to see Rita," he had told his mom.

He was having a fantastic toddler day. A few weeks later, however, was a different story. In his prospective, the day wasn't at all sunshiny, and no matter what his mom did, he wasn't happy. He whined, and pouted and didn't even want the little specialty drink I concoct just for him when he visits.

Jace is two and in the process of learning to deal with his emotions, control his feelings, and learn to be happy even if things don't go to his liking. And I stand and watch, chuckling at his various moods.

It's cute. He's but a tot. His mom is a magnificent teacher, and I have no doubt he is going to grow up to be a delight.

—— THE ESPRESSO FACTOR ——

I can totally relate to what Paul the Apostle wrote when he talked about his own life; even though he tried to do good he continued to be weak in some areas, and he was disappointed in himself.

Some days I find myself acting like an immature toddler. Some days I am moved by my emotions instead of by love and grace. And I have pondered on this long and hard: some of our choices may be lawful and justified but may not be necessary or beneficial in the entire scheme of things.

Some decisions seem logical and totally validated but may not show compassion, and oh how my heart desires to be compassionate.

Alas, I face the disappointment in myself, wishing I had left well enough alone concerning a late sequence of events. I wish I had not reacted. I want a do over so the second time around I could keep my mouth shut. I ponder on the thought that my actions might have hindered an opportunity to have made a new lifelong friend. My heart cannot rejoice.

Grace is not asking for forgiveness after pointing out a flaw. Grace is ignoring the flaw from the start. I had reached another milestone that day. I smiled at myself and relished in that moment of feeling all grown up and mature, all the while knowing I would again find myself right smack dab in another life lesson: learning, right along with Jace, perception in the moment will trick us, not everything is beneficial, and alas, we don't always get our way.

Grace is where love grows.

Practice grace.

Because, grace never disappoints

An Interesting Thing
Happened on
the Way to Sixty

Grandmum may be old, but ain't she grand?

Sometimes I yawn when I hear fortyish-year-old women complain about how their youth has slipped away: about a minute wrinkle or not having the muscles in their derriere to keep it perky and tight or how unattractive it is to have a pooch in the belly.

Sometimes, I fight with my inside voice and decide it to be more favorable to simply listen in silence. I just stand by, chuckling to myself, finding it more advantageous to join in on the less dramatic monologue that runs nonstop in my head.

I think to myself, "listen up kid! Ya' ain't seen nothin' yet."

I want to interrupt and ask if they can see me standing here, old and fighting age on my own terms, or ask if they think I am chopped liver or if I am invisible or if they think I am unsightly and barren of success and worth and productivity.

I have won the battle against trying to explain, choosing to take the high road, deciding to simply be a role model. I will let the younger generations and society watch me win, watch me lead, watch me grow wise and become who I was originally intended to be. For age has its privileges. It also has its responsibilities.

And I take a step back down memory lane to my fortieth year. I was 20 plus years younger than today. At that age, I was smart and rather daring when it came to business. I loved people. I loved God. And at the time, I truly believed I loved life. However, I was a slave to the bathroom scales, wearing a preteen boy jean, and I was afraid of food. I was a workaholic, and a worrier. I had a phobia of introducing myself to other people and found any kind of public speaking extremely difficult.

I lived, on a daily basis, in fear of failing. Not the kind of fear that caused one to sit on the couch and do nothing, but the kind that will drive you to strive for perfection, 24/7.

My story is really no different than most. If truthful, we all struggle with a wanting for something we were never meant to have, reaching for the stars when we aren't equipped, as of yet anyway. We look over the fence at someone else's garden and want roses when our soil is best suited for daisies.

If we're artists, we wish we were better at accounting, or if we are a numbers guru, we daydream about being an athlete. We all want to be thinner, have a rounder bootie, or be more muscular. We don't want to be too tall, but not too short either. We want to be JUST RIGHT.

What we're really saying is we want to live a fairy tale life, like Goldielocks, because we want what we want."

She was looking for just the perfect circumstances to make herself feel comfy and cozy. One could even say that maybe, she was being a little brattish.

We move from one thing to another, never feeling content. If we are not careful we may end up like Hansel and Gretel, seeking out the candy house that leads us into a trap.

Around the fifty-year mark, I began to understand what God's grace was all about. I began to understand what He was trying to show me all along: how to treasure *me* and the gifts I was born with and he taught me how to love others for who they were. With grace came peace and a clearer understanding of my journey. I wondered how I had survived life up to now without it. And for my first forty years, I had not understood that life itself is the journey. I learned that none of us are born all-knowing; none of us take our first breath being 100 percent complete.

At fifty the shackles began to rattle, and I became bolder and less judgmental. Grace for me was the key to unlocking the chains I had unknowingly carried around since before puberty. At fifty, Poppa Bear and I moved to a different state. I attended culinary school. Society told me I was too old, but I found my moxie and pushed through anyway. I graduated top in my class

and discovered that this was what I was born to do. It became
evident at that hour, at that specific juncture of the journey, that
this was what I was made for. Just like a decade before when
I found myself restoring a vintage structure and eventually
opening up a bed-and-breakfast. It was at that time the seed
was planted for culinary school as I hosted guests for dinners
and made specialty desserts and served wine. Each season has a
purpose. In some we plant. In some we water in order to bring
us the season's harvest.

As I grew in grace, I found myself in Rome speaking before
crowds of women at a women's conference. The more I yielded
to grace, the more mercy and benevolence I could offer, not only
to myself but to others; I found more shackles falling from my
soul.

Alas, I began to understand that we are not to yearn for
the journey of the future but it was about experiencing it now.
I began to see that age is not to be feared but to be cherished.

Then it happened one day on my journey to sixty. It was as
if I was Sleeping Beauty. My eyes were opened, and I discovered
just how spectacular my life and my journey had been all along.
I had only fallen asleep to the fact we know in part. We see in
part. And we learn along the way.

——— THE ESPRESSO FACTOR ———

So what is the moral to this real life fairy tale?

We all have a personalized journey. The journey doesn't present itself magically overnight. The journey is not about age or weight, money, prestige, or even a timeline. It's not about living in the same season day after day, year after year.

It's about progression. It's about accepting change. It's about understanding that others have not walked where we've walked.

It's about understanding the forty-year-old moms in no way can understand what it's like to be fifty, and the fiftyish crowd can't go where a sixty-year-old businesswoman has been any more than I can perceive what it's like to walk the journey my eighty-six-year-old mother is on.

It's about granting others grace to find their own path on their own timeline. It's about allowing grace into our lives to change us, encourage us, free us from society's opinions and life's bumps and bruises.

It's about allowing grace to free us from ourselves.

At what age did you begin to wake from your slumber?

Are you learning to walk out your journey without feeling guilty or exasperated about the season you're in?

What can you change now to help you prepare for the journey ahead?

Write your story like only you can and discover just how perfectly wonderful your flawed fairy tale life can be.

9

DON'T LET FEAR KEEP YOU FROM YOUR FUTURE

The Espresso Factor

The Birdcage Was Designed to Keep the Hummingbird from Flying

---

Fear has one agenda. It is to hold us captive.

We have hummingbirds out at the ranch. They come and go as they please, feeding on the wildflowers that voluntarily scatter themselves across our pastures. They can get their daily dose of calories from the flowers we have planted and, yes, from the feeders we diligently keep full of nectar to help them sustain their energetic little bodies as they flitter about like mini, out-of-control helicopter drones.

What would happen if these minute rambunctious feathered fairies were to be confined inside a small canary cage? They, unfortunately, would not survive.

Hummingbirds have extraordinary aviation skills and are capable of flying up, down, sideways, and backward. In fact, they have a need to fly and were made for intricate movement. Most of us would never consider holding such glorious creatures captive, yet, do we not place ourselves in our own jail cell?

I look around. I listen. I see birdcages all about me with doors open wide, welcoming any who dare enter. Unfortunately, it is not birds I see but people inside the aviary. . . . So many human beings, choosing to be there, even fighting for their place, not outside where there is freedom to fly but within the bars, closing the doors, latching themselves tightly inside.

So many, willingly give up their freedom in exchange for a sense of safety instead of taking flight. Bit by bit, they begin to lose their passion and motivation to do what they were born to do: fly.

We've all be there. We've all faced turbulent times. No one is exempt. Right smack dab in the middle of one of those seasons, I recall making a declaration to myself: no matter what happened, I would remain committed to having a strong, steady flight. No matter the storm circling me, I would not crash and burn, but I would seize the day with gusto. Each day I vowed not to back down but to continue moving forward. I drew a line in the sand: I would not allow fear to cage me. I would continue to follow my heart and not my head. I would walk by faith not by sight. I would not cave to my emotions.

I refused to throw my own pity party, even though some days I have gone as far as dialing up the caterer. I would not allow my emotions to dictate my flight.

THE ESPRESSO FACTOR

Sometimes, there is no other way to put it. Life sucks. But we all have choices.

We can either cower from the storm or take flight. We can either run onto the battlefield like Jehoshaphat did with his Israelite army, ready to fight the battle or take shelter inside the cage. Each of us must move forward for a win. There is no winning inside the barred crate.

How we view the storm, however we handle the plight introspectively this year and beyond, will determine how we enter the next season of our life.

There is no doubt in my mind that our attitude is everything. I am certain of this very thing: you were born to fly. Don't give your emotions permission to hold your flight schedule at the will call window. Don't allow fear to cage you. Like the hummingbird, you cannot survive in captivity.

What is your purpose?

Are you intentionally sitting inside the cage or are you ready for takeoff?

What battle have you faced? Did you run into it or sit, trembling in the shadows?

What can you do today in order for you to take flight?

Through the battle, there is purpose.

Dream on Until
the Dream Comes True

And tell yourself stories.

When the clock strikes midnight and Poppa Bear and the two dogs are sleeping soundly, I am here, sitting in the shadows of the night, wide awake. I find myself bright-eyed and bushy-tailed while the rest of the household is on the verge of snoring.

My eyes pop open, and there I am thinking about stuff. You know, those weighty things in life like "I need to lose five pounds off my butt. I'll definitely start that regimen tomorrow." "Was that Croque Monsieur crispy enough?" Or maybe I allow myself to ponder covert names like Chef Bernadette La Blanc, who has crazy scary knife skills and isn't afraid to use them, if I ever, in my second life, would become a street smart undercover agent fighting crime and having a closet full of disguises. I am forever curious about how my text messages get from my iPhone screen to my friend Donna in China, all perfectly typed out within seconds. I speculate what it would be like to speak at the same women's conference Ann Lamott is speaking at or even what it would be like to become an author who has truly wise things to say. Because at night, there are many important things to mull over.

But mostly I find myself in awe of just how magnificent God is. How He directs me, shelters me, helps me bring my heart's desires to fruition all the while giving me the gift of grace. Something else I wonder is, if He keeps the universe on its axis and the sun and moon rise and set at His command, why in the world can't He answer my questions during the day? If He calms the seas, you'd think He could calm my overactive brain when it's gone rogue in the middle of the night. But He doesn't work that way.

He puts us in charge of our own selves. He's not a genie in a bottle, nor is He a puppeteer. He is the Creator. So I sit in the wee hours of the morning deliberating things. And I talk to myself and God.

And sometimes I feel as a child, not different from my two youngest grandkids. They ask questions. Random questions. Just anything that pops into their head. And I smile and I chuckle because they have set for themselves no boundaries.

Sometime back, both Jasper and Ava Kate spent the night with us. Sitting at the little bistro table for breakfast the following morning, this conversation occurred:

"I didn't dream last night," Jasper said in a serious tone.

"You didn't?" I asked with concern in my voice. "I'm sorry. Do you have a lot of dreams?"

"Yes, but not as much as I used to," Jasper replied with a most disappointed sound to his voice.

Ava Kate chimed in, bright-eyed and wearing her usual sassy pants. "Do you know you can tell yourself stories?" she asked.

"Oh my goodness, you can?" I asked. "Wow! Do you tell yourself stories?"

"Yes, when I can't sleep, I talk to myself," she said and then giggled.

And there you have it, folks, simple as a child. Dreaming and allowing themselves to become storytellers. My grandkids are at peace with themselves and the universe.

What happens to us as we grow? We adults call it maturity. How sad actually, that we go from letting our minds wonder with no limitations, and dreaming of awesomeness to come to setting ourselves up with endless boundaries.

I've always been a dreamer, dozing off in the midst of what some might consider noteworthy stuff. I would drift into space during high school science or math class, all the while creating for myself a future that was exciting, adventurous, and thought provoking—one that made me feel brave, kinda like a female Indiana Jones.

There's nothing that will bring you back to earth like a whack on the head with a ruler from an annoyed teacher doing what she thought best but accomplishing nothing more than to embarrass you. This was way back in the day when teachers could surprise you with such discipline and it certainly was not considered a faux pas or abuse. No matter...I refused to let them break my spirit and I never stopped my daydreaming.

This has been my life: Earth to Rita. Earth to Rita. I now live free of that humiliation and have gotten over the shame plenty of arrogant, brazen folks have tried to implant within me. Many of them were simply hoping to jolt me back to reality or possibly attempting to get me to see things from their perspective. You know, trying to make me "normal." But they never seemed to quite get the job done.

Not many years ago, a well-meaning man in a leadership position in a church I attended, proceeded to try to help me understand that I needed to live a more practical life. He bluntly explained to me how I lived with my head in the clouds and that down-to-earth and sensible thinking was much more efficient and prudent. He proceeded to tell me, with love of course, that I lived in a fantasy world, and I needed to be more disciplined with my thoughts and wishes and dreams.

I remember leaving that place, crushed, even as an adult. I crawled into bed and didn't come out for three days. And I wept. My soul had taken a tremendous blow. I lived with a real and raw fact: a knowing that most people did not understand me. And it was a lonely place to be.

I knew I was created to create. For heaven's sake, God Himself is the Creator, and you'll never convince me He didn't have a plan laid out when He spoke and set the world into motion. I am created in His image. I am a creator. Edison was a creator. Henry Ford was a creator. How about Marie Curie, Shakespeare, Frank Lloyd Wright, Rod Stewart, Maya Angelou, and Norah Jones? They are all creators doing what was put inside them to do—to improve someone else's life with medicine, drama, architecture, music, and poetry to heal the soul.

THE ESPRESSO FACTOR

We were all born with that special something. That something only we as individuals can do. Something so incredible it can only be connected to who our own Creator is.

Each one of us has been placed on this earth to do something that shows the world who God is.

You and I both were created for this era, this generation, this cycle of life.

I find it to be incredible—and when I dwell on it long I become breathless and giddy with excitement—knowing He had a plan for all of us from the beginning of time. And I am reassured by His promise that we were made for a time as this; that each of us are connected to Him for this day, for this time, to daydream and create.

We all have that divine purpose.

For some of us it is to build businesses that take constructing from the ground up. Some of us were born to help people no one else can help or maybe to help people free their soul. Many are given the ability to be doctors to help heal the sick, chefs to feed the hungry, actors and dancers to give us entertainment. And yes, even silly, "head in the clouds" me. Especially me, who makes people go what?

Let me encourage you. Let me remind you that it is certainly okay to look at life through the eyes of a child. I dare you. I double dare you. When you can't sleep, be like a child. Be like Jasper that is disappointed he skipped a night of dreaming. Be like Ava Kate; tell yourself a story and see what kind of exploits await your future.

Be like Steven Tyler and dream on because dreams really do come true.

Dare to dream.

Think back to the time you allowed yourself to dream. When was the last time, anyway?

If you are like me and live a life of dreaming, good for you. What's the next crazy, "out of the box" thing you've been pondering in the night hours? Write it down.

If your soul has been wounded by others wanting to crush your creativity, you have to forgive them. Freedom cannot come if you harbor unforgiveness. Let it go.

What is something you've dreamed about doing but were afraid to verbalize it?

Now, grab that pen and begin to write down anything that comes into your brain. It doesn't have to be earth shattering or even make sense, just write it down.

Dream on. Take up your purpose and fly.

10

POSITION YOURSELF

The Espresso Factor

We'll Keep the Light
on for Ya

Be a blazing torch in someone's darkness.

Many years ago now, Poppa Bear and I restored an old boarding house and opened it back up as a bed-and-breakfast. Our guests were mostly weary travelers looking for crisp, cool sheets for their tired bodies, a soft pillow to lay their head, and a grandiose breakfast experience before moving on down the road to the next leg of their journey. We did our best to give them all of these and more.

Some arrived early, taking advantage of our reading room or relaxing while watching old movies. They took advantage of the snack bar stocked with a selection of beverages including hot coffee, fresh baked cookies, and an assortment of other goodies.

Others arrived late, after dark. They would find chocolate mints on their pillow and cookies and bottled water on their nightstand.

We always made sure the porch light was left on, allowing them to see clearly as they made their way up the unfamilar to them walkway, to our front door.

Our life is kinda like that. On any regular ole day, on our life's journey, we will more than likely arrive somewhere we have never been before. The path looks dark and scary. We may need someone to show us the way, be a light so we can see the path before us, and expose the unknown thresholds. Other times we will need to bring our own flashlight, even lighting a torch for someone else struggling in the darkness.

——— THE ESPRESSO FACTOR ———

I've been seeking the light. Looking in the dark places, hoping to bring good to the hidden nooks and crannies of this world. As I go about looking, I find the light in so many things, so many places, so many people.

In fact, I have discovered the light has been here all the time. But to find it, we must keep our eyes open and be willing to see it.

Yep, there's been days when I've felt my torch may be dimming. Times when I held the torch in one hand and paddled upstream with the other, fighting the rough current as the rapids wanted to take me under. But then invariably, there have been times little things have shown up unexpectedly like little rays of sunshine. Bits of hope, unforseen gifts, and sweet surprises come with perfect timing, letting me know the struggle is worth every moment.

There have been times when my coffee estate friends in the Dominican Republic have sent me bags of their coffee beans along with a precious letter, letting me know I was on their mind. Poppa Bear was interviewed by a TV station for a special segment on his wood art. I got to make the host of the show one of my coffee specials. All of this in the same week I received news of my coffee bean sales going up.

You ask me how to find the light? It's everywhere. All we have to do is live with our eyes wide open.

And as I continue my search, as I continue to keep my torch lit, the light in me seems to magnify, expelling more of the darkness, and I enjoy the benefits of being a torch carrier.

It's quite simple, really. Treat others as you would want them to treat you. Feed the hungry, hug the hurting, love those who don't know how to be loved. I find we really do reap what we sow. Sow kindness and receive kindness. Sow sunshine. Reap warmth.

Be the light. Be a torch carrier. Be the kindling that helps ignite the flame so others can see.

We don't own the bed-and-breakfast anymore, but maybe, I can still leave the light on for ya after all.

Have you ever needed someone to light up a path for you or someone to help carry a few of your burdens? It's an incredible feeling knowing someone cares enough to help.

Make an extensive list of ways you can be the light. After the list is complete. Go. Do. It.

Here's an idea. One year I bought blankets for the homeless and gave them out on a cold, windy day. It's easy. Find a way. There's a plethora of ways you can help light up someone's darkness. It's actually one of the best things about the journey.

Share the light and watch the darkness disappear.

Lonely or Empowered

The answer is up to you.

The day presented itself with opportunity. Opportunity for what, you may ask. Anything I wanted.

There is a phrase that I have pondered for some time now. Many use it as a marketing tool, as a slogan, or even as accreditation for themselves: "I empower woman to be the best they can be."

And I wonder if this is even possible.

A few years ago, I started a woman's group I called Coffee Talk. I would cook a light supper and make coffee. I opened up with conversation, deep conversation. I asked questions I hoped would provoke others to ponder.

Because of the Coffee Talk group, many would ask, "So you empower women, right?"

It was inevitable, I suppose, but nonetheless, I hated that question and the assumption leading to it. The only suitable answer was, "Heck, no! I don't have the power to do that."

Amidst my journey and at different junctures along the way, I have had women say they needed a Rita fix. They've wanted to be my bestie. They've hung on to every word I've spoken and waited anxiously for me to unlock their happiness and success.

Given enough time, I would invariably stub my toe, showing all who looked on just how human I really was. And that would be the end of that. I hate pedestals. Because no one has the power to maintain the worthy status.

With that expectation comes failure and waiting on me or anyone for that matter to give you validation and empowerment can only lead to disappointment, disillusionment, and lost friendships. People cannot expect things out of other human beings they have no power to give. It's up to each of us to unleash our own destiny.

——— THE ESPRESSO FACTOR ———

We all have the key within our own selves to unlock our heart's desires. It was given to us while in our mother's womb. A gift from God. We can start businesses, write books, run marathons, lose excess weight and start a nonprofit. Even lead a woman's group called Coffee Talk.

It's up to us as individuals to work on our own confidence, self-esteem, and self-respect. The ball is always in our own court.

I love spending the afternoon shopping in the art district, getting my hair re-pinked, eating a cheese board in a local pub out of a cardboard box. It feels fantastic.

Sometimes, I linger in the pub, making notes about life. Sometimes I ask complete strangers to take pictures of me for my Instagram page, or I meet a new female artist at the local art gallery. I might even buy a piece or two of vintage clothing from my favorite thrift store.

All simple things really. It makes for a peaceful day, a victorious day, an emotionally prosperous day, and it brings peace to my soul.

Because I hold the key to my happiness, my success, my emotional contentment, I don't need an entourage to hold my hand or rely on anyone to pull me along. Only me, myself, and I can make the decision to embrace what destiny has for me.

I alone must learn to trust that God has a plan for me and that the plan is good. No one else can make that decision for me nor can they drag me out of my comfort zone.

How about you? Are you waiting for someone to come along who can empower you?

When was the last time you spent time lollygagging about, entertaining yourself?

Make a list for fun things to do on your own. It doesn't have to be huge. Just take baby steps.

Now, look at the calender and choose a day to start marking off that list.

I hope you find your own tenacity and boldness today to do the very thing you desire to do—even if it's spending the day eating a cheese board out of a cardboard box in a pub in the middle of a hot afternoon.

Please, stop waiting for someone to come along to validate or empower you.

You hold your own power. I hope you use it today.

11

PREPARE FOR TAKEOFF

The Espresso Factor

So You Long for the Preakness

First you train; then you race.

I'm a runner. No, not like a marathon runner or even on the hiking trail kind of runner, but in: I'm a spiritual runner. I am always running the race that is set before me. I'm a "new idea, looking for unique adventures, over the top possibilities every morning," kind of runner.

I simply love testing the waters. I am forever on the lookout for when the next phase of the journey might introduce itself.

I am a runner, not a tippy-toer nor a crawler. I have never been a, "hold on to the handrail until I get my balance" kinda' girl. But instead I'm an "off to the races" woman.

You've heard the old cliché: She was like a racehorse at the gate on race day. Well, that would be me.

A racehorse was born to race. It's in its DNA. And with training, that's what she'll become. However, a horse that is born to race does not run full speed every day all day long. Some days she walks. Some days she gallops at a leisure pace. There are days she runs at full capacity and is clocked. Some days she does nothing more than get a massage and a weighted blanket to ease the stiffness from the tired, sore muscles.

It would be harmful to her destiny if she moved full speed seven days a week. Come raceday, she would be exhausted. Exhaustion causes injury. Her trainer knows what's best for her.

The red French door of Café Paradee had been opened for ten years. It had operated like a well-oiled machine, until it began to spit and sputter.

No matter what kind of oil I used or how often I tended to the gears, it simply was tired. I was doing everything I could think of to fix it. Exhaustion showed up, and I concluded it was time to transition.

It was in the beginning, around my one-year anniversary of opening the café. It was a typical late afternoon in my little paradise. I sat in the reading room, feet up, watching with intrigue through the French doors, as the sparrows splashed about in the cottage garden fish pond. I pondered my success and contentment more than flooded my soul.

I was relishing the moment when an epiphany showed up out of the clear blue; like a wow factor it was. I then knew and understood that this space I was so dearly enchanted with, this leg of my journey in which I had enjoyed great peace, was simply a catalyst to get me where I really needed to be.

That was several years ago, and much water has run under the bridge. I have found that success comes in seasons. We train for the race. And we run and we win. And we rest and we plan and we train some more.

There are days I feel as if I have been corralled. Some days I feel as though I have been halted by a hackamore. I stomp and snort and whinny long and loud like a disgruntled racehorse, as her trainer says, "Not today. Today is not your time."

And my Trainer says, "Not today. Today is not your time."

For I am still in training. Just because one wins the Kentucky Derby does not mean they are ready for the Preakness. Café Paradee was definitely my personal Kentucky Derby. I'm training for my Preakness.

——— THE ESPRESSO FACTOR ———

Sometimes, transitions are slow and the training mundane. There are days I despise the training, and I want to escape the harsh bridle that subdues me. But I wait. I know that the Belmont is yet to come, and I know and understand that for everything there is a season.

All things work together for good. But most of all, I know I was born for such a time as this. And each day is training day until that day comes, and my Trainer removes that cumbersome restraint and says, "Today is the day. Run and win."

How can you relate to my story? What has been your Kentucky Derby? Do you long for your Preakness and Belmont?

What would you have to accomplish that you would consider your Preakness?

What does that look like to you? What are you willing to do to get there? What preparation is necessary?

Because . . . first you train; then you run.

The Day the Squirrel
Went Berserk

All she wanted was freedom.

I love old houses. You know, the vintage ones that have stories to tell. The ones that exude laughter from love shared and life celebrated and have shed tears from scars caused by heartaches. I hear them in my soul. I can see them and feel them when I walk through the door. I've never lived in any structure newer than 1930. The 1920s architecture is my favorite.

Poppa Bear calls it my addiction, maybe even a sickness at times. Some people want to rescue puppies. Me? Well, I want to rescue old houses. I believe there is nothing a little paint, hammer, and nails, extra spakling and a lot of elbow grease can't fix.

My philosophy is that no house is beyond repair. Poppa Bear's is "no house is beyond repair if you have a big enough bank account."

We moved to Ft. Worth and bought my dream home in a historic district. Poppa Bear and I thought we would retire and die in that house. It was my heaven on earth. It was a 1926 French Tudor built by the infamous owner of the Ziegfeld Follies, a theatrical revue production series on Broadway helping to launch Marilyn Miller's career. Did I mention I was in love with this house?

Three pairs of French doors opened to a huge terra cotta veranda which faced a deep front yard that sat back from the main street providing privacy and solitude. Massive, eighty-year-old crepe myrtle trees lined the perimeter of the yard. In springtime, it was a whimsical sight, a place where fairies might reside.

But we didn't have fairies; we had squirrels. These little creatures entertained the dogs and were fun to watch as long as they remained outside frolicking in the yard. Inside the house were four large, incredibly beautiful fireplaces. None of them at the time were useable, except for nesting squirrels. And nest they did.

One thing lead to another until one momma squirrel came down the chimney just like Santa on Christmas Eve. Now, one doesn't expect to catch Santa scampering about the house leaving presents any more than we expected to hear the commotion coming from the back bedroom. The momma squirrel spied me about the time I saw her, and the escapade was on. Up and down the curtains she went, across the bed, back and forth as fast as lighting. I began my own revised jitterbug and squealed like a girl.

The pup was doing his part in trying to corral the loose varmint, only making things worse, and Poppa Bear, well, like always, he kept his senses. Closing off the bedroom, we waited and prayed that this little renegade would find her way back up the chimney.

After what seemed like an eternity, she did just that. And we capped off the entrance she had come down, making sure she would have to find a more suitable place to make a home for her babies.

──── THE ESPRESSO FACTOR ────

Finding herself in a place she was not born to be brought havoc to this momma squirrel. She was not designed to be housed inside a human's home. It would not be healthy for her to live in confinement. She was made to be a creature of nature.

Her playground was to be in my Crepe Myrtles; her food supply falling generously from the giant oak tree in our back yard. Her hammock for napping was to hang from the various hardwoods giving her freedom to watch the sun rise and fall at an easy glance. This momma squirrel could never be content living within boundaries. Boundaries would be her prison. Sometimes, we look for safety in places that can only be our demise later on. Sometimes we are like the momma squirrel; we set unhealthy boundaries for ourselves.

Are you living in freedom? Or are you in lockdown in self-made perimeters? How is that working for you?

Are you content or are you like the momma squirrel, running to and fro in panic mode, trying desperately to find your way out?

What's confining you? An occupation you've outgrown? Could it be fear or jealousy of other people's accomplishments? Maybe it's procrastination or self-doubt. Heck, our prison can be anything keeping us from living the life we were meant to live. What is holding you captive?

Like the squirrel, you were made to live unrestrained and in freedom.

Find your escape route from whatever holds you in bondage, and like the momma squirrel live in freedom. Find an escape route and block the entrance.

Because you were made for freedom.

Father Knows Best

Every. Singe. Time.

I didn't want to share this story. It's private. It's painful.

But here I am doing it anyway because this is part of my journey, and because God has asked me to. And Father knows best.

I am a grandmum of eight. Seven have their roots planted here in our rural America state. The eighth, our Eden, took up residency in heaven at twenty-two months of age. I'm sure she is speaking fluent French by now. She's probably helping Julia Child make everyone's birthday cakes, and I have no doubt she is the star of Paradise Dance Company.

Eden was born the year I opened Café Paradee. She was right smack dab in the middle of everything when we moved into our historical building. I would greet her with a "Bonjour Eden" every morning when she entered the café, and it brought me joy to load her up with as many cookies as her little heart desired. She would grin from ear to ear.

At seventeen months of age, she began to lose her giggles, and she was tired and restless. The doctor's appointments began. A plethora of tests were run. She grew weaker, and we were frightened. The test results came; the most dreaded words any parent could ever hear were spoken: "it's cancer." Eden spent most of her last five months in bed at OU Children's medical center.

Her little body suffered because of chemo. She was picked at and prodded with needles, drugged with harsh, manmade pharmaceuticals to control the pain, and she was fed through a tube. She lost her curly hair, and her rose colored skin took on the color of ash.

Eden surrendered to neuroblastoma at twenty-two months of age. Her last day was spent on machines, surrounded by a team of doctors, hooked up to IVs, slipping into code blue off and on for hours, yet somehow being brought back.

Our hopes and prayers continued. We violently petitioned heaven on her behalf, warring for her health, and for a full recovery.

It was 2:00 p.m. the day after Christmas when she slipped into code blue for the last time. Her mommy and daddy chose to let her go. The machines were unplugged. And the pain came. There is no greater pain.

I've mentioned before that the café had gone through a tremendous transition. It flourished for many years. And then it didn't.

We had issues with lack of help, our town's sliding economy, and the list could certainly go on. I did everything I could to keep it healthy. I was worn out, and the days passed. I worked long and hard with great determination to find a way. And my journey continued.

I was up super early one morning. It was dark outside. I sat on my couch, pleading with God for an answer. Within seconds, it was as if He swooped in, and I was transcended back to Eden's hospital room. I watched from above as the doctors resuscitated her, repeatedly. I saw the doctors work long and hard to fix her. Yet, she could not live. And in an instant, I was back on my couch.

The tears flowed and anger rose up inside.

"How dare you take me through that again," I cried out in frustration and petulance. "This is unfair, and I do not understand."

Then God, with His ever-lasting grace, spoke with words of love and compassion that brought a comfort to my soul: "I've told you over and over to let the café die. Yet you keep trying to resuscitate it. This was the only way I could get you to understand. Eden, if she would have lived, would never have been the same. There would have been lasting damage. But she now truly lives. Café Paradee is the same. You have to let it die, so it can truly live."

I wept from the depths of my soul. And I finally understood. I knew what I must do. I must take the café off life support. And the process continues.

There are some days I want to fight for it, hook it up to IVs, war violently for it to be what it used to be, but that season and the purpose it first had, is past. I need to let it rest in peace, so surly, in the right time, it shall live.

——— THE ESPRESSO FACTOR ———

Life is not fair. We were never promised it would be. It is full of many seasons. There is a time to live and a time to die, a time to laugh and a time to weep.

Have you been resuscitating something that has come to its end? Nurturing something that has been sick for a long while? That may never be healthy again?

What is it you need to let go of so it can live?

Let me encourage you to let it go. Allow yourself to grieve. And watch it live in an entirely different way.

Because Father knows best.

And the Chickadee Must Sing

Welcome Home, Ava Kate, Welcome Home!

She was tiny. Oh, so tiny. Tiny and fragile and as vulnerable as a freshly hatched chickadee. The first time I laid eyes on her, my heart leaped with joy. As I cuddled her close, gratefulness flooded my soul. I knew before she was twenty-four hours old, that this little bundle would be joining our family. The evidence poured in through phone calls laced with tears as our daughter shared how she had begun to speak life over her while she lay in her hospital crib alone.

Touching her, whispering words of destiny and promise and all things good, our daughter Tatum wanted this newborn to know she was loved, even before her very first breath and from the beginning of time, she had a purpose.

Her name is Ava Kate Zeal—a name so very fitting. She is a firecracker of a little girl, headstrong, sharp as a tack, and too big for her britches most of the time. She came to us at two days old and is our number eight grandchild. She joined our family not through a bloodline but simply because she was wanted and loved.

If you are having breakfast at the local diner, you can see her eating her pancakes setting smack dab in the middle of her brother's football team. Did I mention there can be days she's definitely too big for her britches?

From a tiny dancer on production day to coach-pitch softball during summer little league, she lights up our world. There are days she helps me in the café, instructing me on how to make my own signature cookies. She's a gift with a purpose, with a destiny, because God never makes a mistake. And He fixes ours.

—— THE ESPRESSO FACTOR ——

Not all things spectacular and radiant and life changing come to us through ideal conceptions. Sometimes what looks to be a mistake at first is actually just what we needed.

There have been times I knew I had missed the mark, when I'd made poor choices, knowing there could be no turning back. Yet in those times I discovered these situations only gave God ample opportunity to turn my world upside-down with all kinds of goodness.

He loves working on my behalf. No opportunity is too big or too small. Nothing is ever wasted. Through all kinds of circumstances and baggage, an abundance of miraculous gifts can be found.

Stop worrying so much about the muddles and look for the ways in which God shows up. Sometimes it's in the form of someone buying you a cup of coffee. Sometimes, it's a framed picture of you and your old dog given to you by a friend after the old guy has crossed the rainbow bridge.

Sometimes it comes to us as a tiny human chickadee who needs a family, and instantaneously you find you need her as much as she needs you.

Mistakes are nothing more than perception. To find the goodness, sometimes we must change the way we see things. To change our life, we must change our lens to see life through the eyes of God's never ending grace.

Have you felt you've made mistakes that were too big to fix?

Do you still carry the burden around with you?

Is it condemnation that ties you to the old gaffes?

Remember, there is not one human being that escapes life without poor choices, stubbed toes, miscalculations. You are not alone.

Write down the number-one issue you've faced concerning a mistake you've made. Or maybe you've been judgmental toward someone for making a mistake. Write that down too. Write a prayer of forgiveness releasing yourself or others from the past.

Now, write a short thank-you note to God for helping you change your perception lens.

Because a chickadee must sing.

East Bound and Down, Loaded Up and Truckin'

And sometimes we find giants blocking our route.

There I was, sitting behind the wheel of a big rig, 18-wheeler. With one foot on the brake, I released the clutch with smooth, steady precision, engaging the lowest gear. Then I shifted into second, and with nary a hitch, off I went.

I had expected the changing gears part would be more difficult, but to my surprise, it was a breeze. It was a smooth ride and made for a lot of giggles.

Then I woke up. It was quite a disappointment to discover this entire scenario had only been a dream. But did this dream hold a valuable key?

Have you ever seen the classic comedy *Smokey and the Bandit,* featuring Burt Reynolds and Jackie Gleason? Poppa Bear and I saw it back in the day. We thought it was a hoot, so when our local theatre had classic movie night featuring this fun relic, we were all in. The storyline of the movie has cops chasing trucks hauling illegal beer, fast cars playing the decoy, a runaway bride, and Cletus the basset hound, all taking side roads, hitting dead ends, and experiencing a fender bender or two along the way. We laughed at all the craziness until we almost peed our pants.

Of course, it's always fun and games while watching this kind of silliness on the big screen. It's easy to laugh out loud from the comfort of a theater, but when we find ourselves traveling the bumpy roads of life: dealing with a few crash and burns of our own, or until our plan comes upon massive roadblocks, it is another story.

When we find ourselves facing giants, we have to become smarter, tougher, and more tenacious than our circumstances. We must outwit fear and intimidation. When things don't go our way, we've got to be flexible, remembering there's more than one route to get us where we need to be.

Now, I'm not advocating anything like breaking the law by running shotgun for illegal contraband. What I am saying is sometimes our navigation is askew, and we need to make an adjustment.

For every dream we carry, for every plan, for every blueprint there will be an obstacle . . . a giant hoping to stop us from completing our assignment. There will be roadblocks to bust through, detours to take, and extra hours of fortitude needed.

——— THE ESPRESSO FACTOR ———

There it was, a land with great farm ground: fertile soil, lush orchards, vibrant vineyards, and flowing fresh rivers, all for the Israelites taking. But when they peered across the fence at the giants, they ran with their tails between their legs.

They had convinced themselves they were not capable of living anywhere but the wilderness. They saw themselves as small and worthless, no better than insects in the sight of the behemoths that stood before them. Therefore, they spent the rest of their lives living in a wasteland.

All but two courageous men who happened to believe all things are possible. Joshua and Caleb said, "we can do this." The rest died, forfeiting their dream of the promised land for familiarity, complacency, and apathy.

There will always be giants in the land: cyclopean problems waiting to be solved, obstacles that need to be overthrown and fear to be faced, if you live with your purpose in mind.

Please, don't allow the giants to tell you, you are not capable. Don't stand peering across the fence while your promised land is waiting for you.

I have faced those giants more than once in my life, and it can seem paralyzing to say the least. But standing in the shadows while others live out loud has never been appealing to me. And I have found my fortitude in God.

Because we all should be East bound and down, loaded up and truckin'. We're gonna do what they say can't be done.

Find God and you'll find grace!

About the Author

Rita spends most of her days in a rural town in Oklahoma, inside her coffee shop, Café Paradee. Her days are filled with real life Coffee Talk stories as she plays the role of barista, bakes cookies, and experiences her own Espresso Factor encounters as people come and go, ordering cookies, sipping espresso drinks, and, most often, simply needing an emotionally safe, friendly space and a listening ear to talk out life issues.

Rita cultivated Café Paradee from a seed that was planted as she braved the culinary world: a world filled with youth, and an overabundance of testosterone, laced with arrogance and disdain towards women and the middle aged. When you put those two together, it sets up a scenario that could have easily led to failure.

Rita, believing all things are possible and that a God idea trumps failure, graduated from culinary school at age fifty, with high marks. A couple years later, Rita launched Café Paradee, a French lunch eatery, right smack dab in the middle of "chicken fried steak, gravy, and apple pie cowboy" country; it worked, because it was a God idea.

After several years, she downsized, making the café into a simple, homey, European-style, "come in and linger, let's have a chat" coffee shop, because it was God's plan. The time she spent cooking and serving lunches is now spent with the people who walk in through her red French door. And this makes her smile.

Rita loves to tell her story of chains of shyness to freedom, of being an average D high school student to becoming an entrepreneur: of her fear of public speaking to speaking at women's conferences.

She knows without a doubt, when God's plan for your life is given a chance, nothing can derail it. She will also tell you that, "you alone, are the one responsible for giving His plan a chance, and you must believe." She is living proof.

She laughs out loud when she says, "simply be who you were created to be. You were made a designer model. Be excited about that."

She is an authentic example of this as she goes about her days loving her pink hair, showing off her full sleeve tattoo, and boldly telling the story behind the art.

Rita is married to her handsome cowboy, Neil, aka Poppa Bear, is a mom to three innovative children, a grandmum to eight exceptional grandchildren, and a human mom to a humorous and entertaining Chinese Crested.

Rita is available for speaking engagements and can be reached via her email, rita@ritabarney.com

For more of the Espresso Factor follow Rita on Instagram, Facebook, and on her website, at ritabarney.com.

CPSIA information can be obtained
at www.ICGtesting.com
Printed in the USA
LVHW021031290721
694023LV00007B/1155